AF736762

The Effects of Structural Relations on Transfer

Originally published in 1970 *The Effects of Structural Relations on Transfer* follows on from the investigation reported in the first volume *Thinking in Structures*. It deals with four problems:

1. How far is it true that learning is accelerated by tackling the more difficult tasks first?
2. Do learning situations largely under the learner's control increase ability to learn large mathematical groups?
3. Does Structural learning take over from Stimulus/Response Association learning as the material becomes more complex?
4. Are there age-differences in the amount of difficulty experienced with material taken in different orders?

Some valuable answers are elicited, and the results are considered for their implication in actual classroom practice. Today it can be read in its historical context.

The Effects of Structural Relations on Transfer

Psychological Monographs on Cognitive Processes,
Volume Two

Z. P. Dienes and M. A. Jeeves

Routledge
Taylor & Francis Group
LONDON AND NEW YORK

First published in 1970
by Hutchinson Educational

This edition first published in 2026 by Routledge
4 Park Square, Milton Park, Abingdon, Oxon, OX14 4RN

and by Routledge
605 Third Avenue, New York, NY 10158

Routledge is an imprint of the Taylor & Francis Group, an informa business

© 1970 Z. P. Dienes and M. A. Jeeves
© 2026 Bruce Dienes and M. A. Jeeves

All rights reserved. No part of this book may be reprinted or reproduced or utilised in any form or by any electronic, mechanical, or other means, now known or hereafter invented, including photocopying and recording, or in any information storage or retrieval system, without permission in writing from the publishers.

Publisher's Note
The publisher has gone to great lengths to ensure the quality of this reprint but points out that some imperfections in the original copies may be apparent.

Disclaimer
The publisher has made every effort to trace copyright holders and welcomes correspondence from those they have been unable to contact.

For Product Safety Concerns and Information please contact our EU representative GPSR@taylorandfrancis.com. Taylor & Francis Verlag GmbH, Kaufingerstraße 24, 80331 München, Germany

A Library of Congress record exists under ISBN: 9780090993000

ISBN: 978-1-041-34998-3 (hbk)
ISBN: 978-1-003-79553-7 (ebk)
ISBN: 978-1-041-35002-6 (pbk)

Book DOI 10.4324/9781003795537

Psychological Monographs on Cognitive Processes

VOLUME TWO

THE EFFECTS OF STRUCTURAL RELATIONS ON TRANSFER

Z. P. DIENES

Professor of Mathematics Learning
Sherbrooke University, Canada

&

M. A. JEEVES

Professor of Psychology
University of Adelaide, South Australia

HUTCHINSON EDUCATIONAL

HUTCHINSON EDUCATIONAL LTD
178–202 Great Portland Street, London W1

London Melbourne Sydney Auckland
Bombay Toronto Johannesburg New York

First published 1970

The work reported in this book was carried out at Adelaide, when Professor Dienes was a member of the staff of Adelaide University.

© Z. P. Dienes and M. A. Jeeves 1970

This book has been set in Times printed in Great Britain on Smooth Wove paper by Anchor Press, and bound by Wm. Brendon, both of Tiptree, Essex
ISBN 0 09 099300 4

For Sir Frederic Bartlett

whose pioneering researches in bodily and mental skills have significantly stimulated and guided the experimental study of thinking.

In honour of his eightieth birthday.

Contents

PREFACE 11

1 INTRODUCTION 13

2 ON MATHEMATICAL GROUPS 19
Introduction 19
Klein group and the cyclic 4-group 22
The 5-group 25
The cyclic group with six elements 26
The mathematical group with seven elements 29
The cyclic group with nine elements 30
The direct product 9-group 31
Relationships between the structures used 33
Generation of structures by rules 36

3 THE EXPERIMENTAL DESIGN AND THE PERFORMANCE MEASURES USED 40
Techniques used 40
Administration of the task 43
Equations to be solved in each task 47
Subject characteristics 51
The experimental design 52
The dependent variables 54

Scores:

(*a*) *The A Operation score* 54

(*b*) *The Equation score* 54

(*c*) *The B Operation score* 55

Indices:

(*a*) *Position index* 56

(*b*) *Instance index* 56

(*c*) *Frequency index* 56

(*d*) *Index of operationality* 58

(*e*) *Matrix variance index* 58

APPENDICES TO CHAPTER 3

I Front of machine *facing page* 48

II Programme square in back of machine *facing page* 49

III Individual index matrices 58

4 TRANSFER 60

Some relationships between the structures embodied in the experimental tasks 60

Methods of assessing degree of transfer between structures 65

What is being transferred? 66

1. *Some role interpretations of transfer* 67

2. *The group matrices labelled according to the role interpretations* 71

3. *Some S-R theory interpretations of transfer* 81

4. *The group matrices labelled according to triad learning interpretations* 81

5. *Task difficulty assessed in S-R terms* 88

The effects of treatment on performance 89

1. *Comparison of performances on the 3-group and 5-group, depending on order of presentation* 89

2. *Performances on the 5-group and 6-group compared* 93

3. *Performances on the 7-group under different treatments* 94

4. *Performances on the 9- and 9A-groups compared* 95

Comparing the performances of adults and children 96

1. *Differential effects of the 'fittingness' of various structural relationships* 96

2. *Adults and children compared on the 3-, 6- and 9-groups* 97
3. *Treatments compared* 98
4. *Adults and children compared on 9A-group* 98
5. *Distribution of 'successes' and 'failures' amongst adults and children* 108
Salient points from the chapter on transfer 110

5 PSYCHOLOGICAL IMPLICATIONS 112
Differential effects of fittingness of symbolisation to structures 123
A possible theoretical model 128
Transfer effects 132

6 EDUCATIONAL IMPLICATIONS 135

REFERENCES 148

Preface

The experiments reported in this monograph developed out of our earlier studies reported in *Thinking in Structures* (1965). Four particular aspects of these experiments called for clarification. First, how far could we go with our so-called 'deep-end philosophy' (that is, of accelerating learning on a series of tasks by giving the more difficult ones first)? Second, could children and adults learn even larger mathematical groups if suitably embodied and presented in learning situations largely under the learner's own control? Third, would our suspicion of the emergence, with tasks of increasing complexity, of 'structural learning' as distinct from 'S–R association learning', be confirmed or not? And fourth, would different kinds of relationships between structures tend to present differing amounts of difficulty at different stages of development? Each of these questions has been answered with varying degrees of certainty in this monograph, and in addition some of the salient features of the psychological model, which is ultimately going to account satisfactorily for such complex learning, have begun to emerge. Once again we have indulged in a little controlled extrapolation and speculation as we have tried to see possible implications of our results for educational practices in the classroom.

We are indebted to several of our colleagues for their continuing interest in our work and for their critical consideration of it at various stages. Dr R. H. Thouless spent some months in the Psychology Department at Adelaide when the preliminary analyses of the results were taking place, and we are pleased to acknowledge the many helpful comments made by him at that stage. In particular the formula we used for making allowance for chance performance on several of our behavioural measures comes directly from him. At a later stage Sir Frederic Bartlett read the whole book in draft form and offered us helpful and encouraging suggestions. Mindful of his influence upon our work, both formally and informally, it gives us great pleasure to dedicate this monograph to him on his eightieth birthday.

We also wish to thank Columbia University who generously arranged for us to work together in New York in May, 1966, thus helping us to surmount some of the problems which arise when two authors are trying to write up a joint project even though their present places of work are 12,000 miles apart. For the latter part of the time when this work was being written up, one of the authors (M.A.J.), was in receipt of a grant from the Australian Research Grants Committee. The South Australian Education Department has continued to give us every assistance in allowing children in their schools to participate in our experiments, and in this regard we are particularly grateful for the help given by Mr E. W. Golding, Headmaster, and Mr F. R. N. Williams, Deputy Headmaster, of Cowandilla Demonstration School. Finally, we warmly acknowledge the invaluable assistance given by our technical staff, research assistants and clerical staff, Mr Bela Parkanyi, Mrs Shirley Mussared, Mr Peter Young, Mrs Marjory Abbott and Mrs Margaret Blaber, without whose help the project could not have been completed.

Z. P. DIENES
Adelaide M. A. JEEVES

1

Introduction

When we try to sort out what is happening in our environment with a view to predicting what is going to happen next, we think. In order to make such predictions, we construct models with various properties. Some of these models are extremely simple, others very complex. They are not, of course, part of the phenomenal world, but are constructs to make sense of our experience. Furthermore, they are susceptible to continuous change in the light of new evidence. Scientists are not the only individuals who make use of models; every living organism constructs them in order to orientate itself in an often hostile environment. Scientists, however, make use of extremely complex models in sophisticated ways, and are thereby enabled to make predictions that surprise the layman.

The problem arises of determining when and how such models are constructed. What, in fact, do we mean when we say that a person has constructed a model? In order to bring the problem into the field of experimental psychology, some behavioural criterion of the possession or lack of possession of such models must be found. The problem of finding criteria which would be generally acceptable to most psychologists has not been solved. We suggest, however, that some steps towards an eventual solution can be taken by an extension of the use of the techniques described in our previous study.*

Care must be taken to distinguish carefully between observable events (in the case of psychology, 'behaviour'), and the constructs which are supposed to 'explain' such observable events. By the word 'explain' nothing causal is intended. The word merely means that we are attempting to classify observable events in such a way as to make it possible to predict certain events or classes of events from the knowledge that certain other events have occurred. For any such set of events a number of different 'explanations' might be given. It cannot be said

* *Thinking in Structures*, 1965, by the same authors.

that one of these is 'true' while the others are not. Some will merely predict correctly more often than others. The models that enable us to predict most accurately in the largest number of cases are the ones that we shall finally keep, until such time as another, more efficient predicting mechanism turns up. In the study of thinking, most of our predicting models will consist of sentences such as:

'This subject is in possession of such and such a concept, or of such and such a structure'

By such a statement we shall mean that, if the subject is placed in a certain type of environment, he is likely to behave in a certain kind of way. The type of environment considered experimentally is inevitably limited by the physical constraints imposed by experimental conditions and considerations of time. All we shall really be able to say at the end of our experiments is that subjects are likely to behave in certain ways in the very limited and carefully circumscribed environments which we have experimentally controlled. What will happen when these conditions are relaxed can be the subject of further experiments, but for the moment remains a matter of opinion.

What do we mean when we say 'Take the first turning to the right', and assume that the person to whom we are saying it 'understands'? Such 'understanding' involves the conjunctive use of 'concepts' (i.e. rudimentary predicting mechanisms) such as (1) first, (2) turning, and (3) right. By 'understanding' we mean that

(a) provided we have given the person to whom we speak sufficient motivation to follow our instructions, and

(b) provided we have put him in a fairly large number of situations of taking the first turning to the right'

we can predict what this person will do; and that in the majority of cases we shall have predicted correctly. So 'understanding' the instruction to 'take the first turning to the right' is not part of the phenomenal world, but is a construct, which enables us to make correct predictions (within certain probability limits) about how any person of whom it is true will behave in certain situations.

When we attempt to predict in our usual environment, we normally do so as a result of taking account of a number of different variables. It would therefore be quite unrealistic to create an artificial environment for experimental purposes in which there was only one variable on which the subject could base his predictions. At least two, if not more, variables should be included, in order to approximate to the real situations in which we find ourselves 'thinking'. The ways in which the combinations of the experimental variables determine the outcome to be predicted by the subject must be quite unknown to him at the outset. For this reason, relationships that are not normally encountered must be used. On the other hand, the relationships to be learned by the subject must be 'learnable' within the limited time available for the experiment. In order to study the effect on 'model construction' of progressively increased complexity, the situations in which the relationships are embodied must be such that the degree of complexity can easily be varied, so that it, too, can be used as an experimental variable. The sets of relationships must themselves be in clearly definable relationships to each other. Using the word 'structure' to indicate any set of relationships, what we are saying is that the progressively more complex structures to be learned by subjects must themselves stand in definable relationships to each other, such as inclusion, overlapping, identity, disjointness, etc. These relationships can then serve as further experimental variables.

Hitherto, most experimental psychologists have only studied the effects of such relationships at the perceptual level. One of our purposes is to extend such studies to the conceptual level, and investigate to what extent there are any parallels between the findings at the two levels.

It seems reasonably evident that the mathematical structures known as 'groups' are likely to satisfy our requirements. In fact, our earlier experiments showed that the use of mathematical groups made possible an analysis of the experimental results which gave the experimenters considerable insight into the cognitive processes underlying behaviour. The use of groups has therefore been extended from 2-by-2 and 4-by-4 structures to groups with as many as nine elements. The resulting complexity of the task entailed considerable mechanisation. Only in this way was there any possibility of recording in sufficient detail the responses of the subjects as they worked. This involved the construction of an electrical machine to simulate the experimenter, the output of which was fed directly into a card-punching machine. The data thus recorded could then be processed and analysed on the computer.

The way in which mathematical groups can be used to create a 2-variable predicting problem is as follows. An initial stimulus is provided, which symbolises one of the elements of the group. The subject is told that there are a certain number of stimuli. The actual number will depend on the number of elements in the group being used. The subject is also told that he can use the same symbols as operators as are being used as stimuli; and that these will operate on the 'state of the game', which is represented by the stimulus currently present. This stimulus, together with the operator selected by the subject, will determine the next stimulus to be presented. The operation involved is, of course, the binary operation defining the group being used. For example, there might be three stimuli, A, X, and Y. Let us say that

A used as an operator leaves the same stimulus there as was there before.

X used as an operator replaces stimulus A by stimulus X
replaces stimulus X by stimulus Y
replaces stimulus Y by stimulus A

Y used as an operator replaces stimulus A by stimulus X
replaces stimulus X by stimulus A
replaces stimulus Y by stimulus X

It will be clear to the mathematical reader that we have 'embodied' in a prediction game the structure of a group with three elements. The use of more complex structures in similar situations should now be evident.

In the previous round of experiments it became clear that, when a subject was given more than one task of this general type, the relationships between the embodied structures had an effect on the transfer of learning and on the strategies used, as also did the order in which the tasks were presented. This raised the more general question of how the relationships between structures affected the successive learning of the structures. We found ourselves considering the conditions under which a structure already learned in one situation would be detected, when embedded in another, wider situation. It became clear, for example, that the learning of the 2-group in the last round of experiments had an effect on the learning of the 4-group, in which the 2-group is always embedded.

We knew, from the previous study, that in some situations it was advantageous to begin the learning with a complex rather than with a simple task, assuming both tasks had to be learned. The question was how complex the first task could become and still confer a positive transfer effect when the performance on this task and on a second simpler task were considered together. In other words, what was the optimum complexity of the initial task in a series, to achieve the greatest efficacy of learning over the series as a whole? In the present series of experiments we were able to use tasks embodying groups with three, four, five, six, seven and nine elements respectively, and to study where the optimum complexity lay by varying the order in which the tasks were performed in the different experimental groups.

By the judicious use of successive applications to the same subject of series of these tasks, we can study the differential effects-on-performance of the various relationships between the structures embodied in the tasks. For example, some of these groups are embedded in each other; whilst others, such as the 6-group and the 9-group (i.e. both 9-groups), overlap, having the 3-group in common. Some of the structures only overlap in that they all have a neutral element, for example, the 3-, 5-, 7-groups. There are other, possibly more striking, relationships between the members of this same series, which can perhaps be given the name 'generalisations' or 'recursions'. The 5-group is an immediate generalisation of the 3-group, so that no complications owing to differences in parity enter into the relationship between the 3- and the 5-group, as would be the case between the 3- and the 4-group. Similarly, a further immediate generalisation takes us to the 7-group. The relationships between the groups in which the number of elements is a prime number are in a sense 'pure', and not clouded by other relationships that might become more apparent to subjects working on problems embodying these groups.

In the 4-group there are only sixteen combinations to learn. From our earlier experiments it was evident that some subjects were able to learn these combinations entirely by rote. Other subjects, indeed the majority of them, had already been seemingly forced into a coding system, and filled in by means of this whenever short-term memory failed them. In the present study we set ourselves to ask what would happen if the tasks were now made so complex that short-term memory alone was never sufficient to cope with the load imposed by the task.

As in *Thinking in Structures,* we have again attempted to design our experiments in order to learn something more of the sort of cognitive development which takes place between the ages of eleven and twenty. For this reason the whole design, aimed primarily at studying the effects of certain structural relationships upon the transfer of learning, was administered to equal numbers of university students and eleven-year-old schoolchildren.

Since we focus attention on our treatment of the results, and subsequently discuss the differential effects on performance of certain structural relationships existing between the mathematical groups, we felt it necessary to give a fairly detailed exposition of precisely what these relationships are and of just how the mathematical groups embody them. Accordingly, the reader will find Chapter 2 given over to an attempt to familiarise the non-mathematical reader with the basic mathematical notions utilised in later chapters.

2

On mathematical groups

Introduction

A group is a simple mathematical structure, applicable in a large variety of mathematical fields, as well as in modern physics, chemistry and crystallography, to mention only a few subjects. In abstract terms, a group is a set of elements in which a binary operation is defined as obeying certain conditions. By 'binary' is meant simply that to any two elements of the set, taken in a given order, corresponds another element of the set. An element may also be combined with itself, and performing the binary operation on these 'two' elements will also yield an element.

From a less abstract standpoint, a group describes certain properties of sets of events which we might come across in real life. For example, the set of displacements within any closed space or surface, or within the whole of space, form a group, as long as all displacements which begin and end at the same place are considered identical displacements. All displacements from a point A to a point B, however tortuous or however straight, would be said to be representations of the displacement which takes one from A to B. The binary operation which immediately suggests itself is the composition of displacements. If the displacement (A to B) is combined with another displacement (B to C), the binary operation can associate to this pair of displacements, *in that order,* the displacement (A to C). An even simpler example would be the turning of a wheel. If we turn a wheel through a certain angle, clockwise or counter-clockwise (but we must state which way), and then, from the position reached, turn the wheel through a further angle, it is clear that we could have obtained the final position of the wheel from the original one by a single turn. Combining two rotations into a single one is another example of a binary operation. The reader can no doubt think of a great many more.

An establishment of a binary operation does not in itself give us a group. The binary operation must be of a certain kind, it must obey certain rules. One of the requirements is that there should be among the set of elements a neutral or unit element, such that

(any element A) combined with (neutral element) yields (element A)

in either order. And this must be so for all elements of the set.

Another requirement is that to every element should correspond an inverse element. An inverse of an element is such that, if you combine the element with it, the binary operation yields the neutral element.

There is yet a third condition, the associative property. For any three elements of the set, say A, B and C, it must be true that:

the element arising out of (A and B) combined with the element C must be the same element as
the element A combined with the element arising out of (B and C).

All these conditions are met, both in displacements and in turning the wheel. The neutral element in the first case is a displacement which starts and finishes in the same place, and in the second case it is turning the wheel a full circle (or several full circles). The inverse of a displacement (A to B) is the displacement (B to A), because

(A to B) combined with (B to A) yields (A to A)

which is the neutral displacement. The inverse of turning the wheel through a certain angle one way is turning the wheel through the same angle the other way. As for the associative property, it is clear that

{(A to B) combined with (B to C)} combined with (C to D) yields the same displacement as
(A to B) combined with {(B to C) combined with (C to D)}.

In both cases, the series of displacements is equivalent to the displacement (A to D). The same can be shown to be true in turning the wheel.

The examples given so far, of sets of situations which have the properties of mathematical groups, consists of sets of elements infinite in number. After one has named any finite number of elements, there are always some left over. There are, however, situations, describable by groups in which there are only a finite number of elements. For example, we can imagine a wheel which comes to a stop after a 120° turn in either sense, say, through a locking device. In this situation we can have the elements:

(1) one 120° turn clockwise
(2) one 120° turn counter-clockwise
(3) no turn

We have to introduce a neutral element, in this case the 'do nothing' element (3), so as to obey the conditions set out for mathematical groups. In any case, if there is to be a binary operation which describes the results of combining the turns, there must be an element corresponding to any pair of elements. For example, there must be an element which is equivalent to the succession of (1) and (2), and this is what (3) is. So (1) is the inverse of (2), and (2) is the inverse of (1). Of course, (3) is the inverse of (3), the neutral always being its own inverse.

It will be seen that the following relationships hold between the elements:

(1) with (1) yields (2)	(1) with (2) yields (3)	(1) with (3) yields (1)
(2) with (1) yields (3)	(2) with (2) yields (1)	(2) with (3) yields (2)
(3) with (1) yields (1)	(3) with (2) yields (2)	(3) with (3) yields (3)

This structure can also be represented by adding numbers whose remainders after division by three are either zero or one or two. The reader should make three collections of numbers: those which are divisible by three (the zero numbers); those which have the remainder one, when divided by three; and those which have the remainder of two, when divided by three. He will find that, if he adds two of the numbers which have remainder one, he will get a number which has the remainder of two. This corresponds to (1) with (1) yielding (2). Conversely, if he adds two numbers whose remainders are two, he will get a number whose remainder is one. This corresponds to (2) with (2) yielding (1). If he adds a number from the remainder-one class to a number in the remainder-two class, he will get a number from the zero class. This is the same as saying that (1) with (2) yields (3), which in this case is the zero or neutral element.

In the experiment that was conducted, one was actually taken as the neutral element; the zero corresponded to the clockwise, and two corresponded to the counter-clockwise, move. This meant that the neutral element was not the first symbol on the dial on the machine. It was the second one up the series of positions on the panel, and the 'matrix' which the subjects had to learn was as follows:

	A	N	X
A	X	A	N
N	A	N	X
X	N	X	A

Here the 'matrix' is simply a 3-by-3 table of the outcomes yielded by the pairs obtained by taking one from the first row and one from the first column.

Klein group and the cyclic 4-group

The Klein group, which has four elements, can be thought of in a number of ways. For example, we can think of any two elements, each of which has two possible ways of occurring. There will, of course, be four possible situations: A and B are on, A is on and B is off, A is off and B is on, A is off and B is off. These are the four states of the game. There are also four changes of these states: change A, change B, change both A and B, and change neither A nor B. All this can be represented by two light switches, the left switch controlling the left-hand side of the room and the right switch the right-hand side of the room. Then the room can be in four different states. The room can be quite dark; the left can be dark and the right can be light; the left can be light and the right can be dark; both sides can be light. The possible operations in this game are: turning the left switch, turning the right switch, turning both switches, turning no switch. The way these operations combine forms the structure known in mathematics as the Klein group. For example, changing A followed by changing both A and B is equivalent to changing B, because A will have been changed twice, and the net effect is that of changing B. Again, changing A and B followed by changing A and B is equivalent to changing nothing, because we have changed them both twice. This, then, is the outcome-table for the structure known as the Klein group:

	A	B	AB	N
A	N	AB	B	A
B	AB	N	A	B
AB	B	A	N	AB
N	A	B	AB	N

Besides the Klein group, there is another group with four elements, the cyclic 4-group. This describes a situation which is generated by any event which, repeated four times, restores the original state of affairs. For example, right angle turns would generate such a group, or quarter-hour intervals elapsing to restore the original number of minutes past the hour. With right angle turns, for example, we could introduce the following elements:

(1) one right angle turn clockwise
(2) one half turn (either way, of course)
(3) one right angle turn counter-clockwise
(4) one full turn, or 'no turn', as may be preferred.

Doing a half turn and then following by a clockwise quarter turn is clearly equivalent to having done one counter-clockwise quarter turn. So we could say that

(2) with (1) will yield (3)

The whole outcome table of the cyclic 4-group is given below.

	1	2	3	4
1	2	3	4	1
2	3	4	1	2
3	4	1	2	3
4	1	2	3	4

It will be seen that it is a totally different table from the one given for the Klein group, although there are some interesting similarities. It will be easier to compare them if we reproduce the Klein group table, calling A=1, B=2, A–B=3, and N=4 (this being the neutral in each case):

	1	2	3	4
1	4	3	2	1
2	3	4	1	2
3	2	1	4	3
4	1	2	3	4

It can now easily be seen that there are just four outcomes that are different in the two matrices, in which cases the outcomes (2) and (4) are interchanged; this means that in the Klein table all elements combined with themselves yield the neutral element, yet this is only so for two of the elements in the other group. Also it will be seen that in the Klein group we have

(1) with (2) as well as (2) with (1) will yield (3)
(1) with (3) as well as (3) with (1) will yield (2)
(2) with (3) as well as (3) with (2) will yield (1)

i.e. out of any pair taken out of the triad [(1), (2), (3)], where the numbers of the pair are different, the outcome is the third member of the triad. This is a comfortably symmetrical situation, which may well have a lot to do with the relative ease of learning the Klein group structure as compared with the structure of the cyclic 4-group. In the latter, two of the pairs will yield the third member of the triad, but not the third pair, i.e. the first and the last of the statements made for the Klein group *remain true* for the cyclic 4-group, but it is *not true* that

(1) with (3) as well as (3) with (1) will yield (2),

because now they yield (4), i.e. the neutral element. The effect of this difference in structural symmetry was studied in the last series of experiments, and a significant tendency towards complete symmetry was noted, even though no experimental evidence was provided in that direction.

Another important difference between the two structures is that one of them is cyclic and the other is not. 'Cyclic' means that there is at least one element in the group which, combined with itself a varying number of times, yields all the elements of the group. This is clearly true of the cyclic group with four elements, since for example

$$(1).(1)=(2), \quad (1).(1).(1)=(3), \quad (1).(1).(1).(1)=(4)$$

The reader should verify that the element (3) is equally suitable for this exercise, whereas the elements (2) and (4) are not.

It is, however, sufficient for there to exist just one such element, out of which all elements of the group can be *generated*, for the group to be termed cyclic.

It will be reasonably evident that the Klein group is not cyclic, because whichever element we start with, when we combine this element with itself, we obtain the neutral element (see table); if we go on to combine the neutral element with the original element again, we get back to the original element. We can never reach the other two. (If, however, we allow ourselves the luxury of two generators, we can then generate all the elements. The table on page 23 does, indeed, show how this can be done, starting with the generators A and B.)

A schematic representation by means of arrows will perhaps make the matter even clearer.

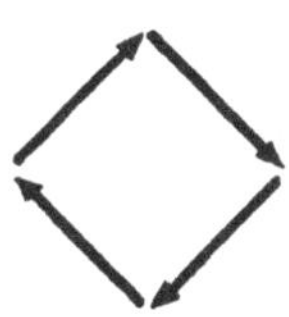

schema for cyclic group

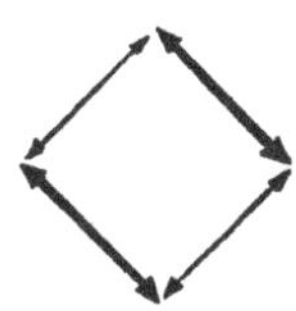

schema for Klein group

The elements of the cyclic group can be enumerated schematically as

$\rightarrow \quad \rightarrow\rightarrow \quad \rightarrow\rightarrow\rightarrow \quad \rightarrow\rightarrow\rightarrow\rightarrow$; (1), (2), (3), (4)

The elements of the Klein group need two kinds of generators, and can be enumerated, for example as

$\rightarrow$	$\rightarrow\rightarrow$	$\rightarrow\rightarrow$	$\rightarrow$
(1)	(4)	(3)	(2)

The 5-group

This can best be embodied in a circle with five points on it, A, B, C, D, and E. If we think of the basic ways we can move around the circle, we find we can take one step round from one point to the next, either clockwise or counter-clockwise; or two steps round from one point to the next-but-one, either clockwise or counter-clockwise. This gives us four moves, and by means of these moves we can go anywhere we please from any starting-point. If we also want to be able to stay where we are, we have to add the no-move, or neutral move. This gives us five moves in all: stay-where-you-are (N), one step clockwise (A), two steps clockwise (B), one step counter-clockwise (X), two steps counter-clockwise (Y). The stay-where-you-are could, of course, be replaced by going-all-the-way-around, which has exactly the same effect. The mathematical group of five elements has the same structure as the relationships between these moves. For example, if we take two clockwise and one counter-clockwise, we might as well have taken one clockwise, or if we take one clockwise and one clockwise, this is equivalent to taking two clockwise. These relationships are described in the 5-by-5 table below:

	B	A	N	X	Y
B	X	Y	B	A	N
A	Y	B	A	N	X
N	B	A	N	X	Y
X	A	N	X	Y	B
Y	N	X	Y	B	A

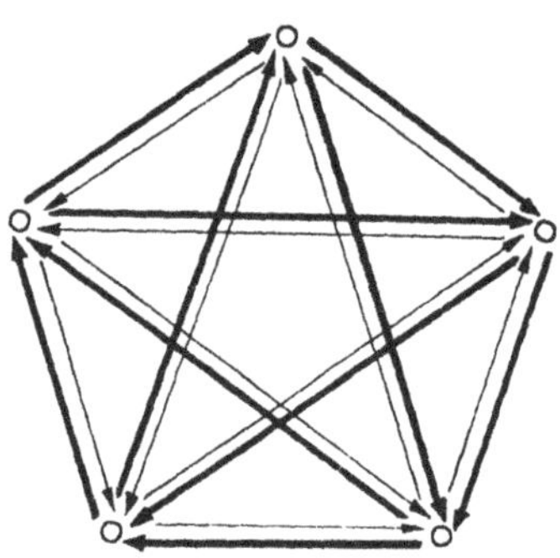

The cyclic group with six elements

This group is obtained in exactly the same way as the previous one, except that six points are marked off on the circle. We can now make the following moves: We can move clockwise one or clockwise two, counter-clockwise one or counter-clockwise two; but we can also move three. In this new move, it doesn't matter whether we move clockwise or counter-clockwise because we shall get to the same place. The sixth move is, of course, the no-move, or the all-the-way-around move.

The relationships between these moves gives us the structure known as the cyclic group with six elements. (There is another group with six elements, which is not cyclic.) It will be remembered that by 'cyclic' is meant that the group can be generated from just one of its elements. In this case, if we take the one clockwise or the one counter-clockwise move and do it often enough, we are able to generate all the moves in the game. If we look back to the mathematical group of five elements, we shall find that this is true also in that case. The clockwise or the counter-clockwise move in that game will generate all the moves in that game.

Here is the outcome-table for the cyclic 6-group:

	H	Y	X	N	A	B
H	N	A	B	H	Y	X
Y	A	B	H	Y	X	N
X	B	H	Y	X	N	A
N	H	Y	X	N	A	B
A	Y	X	N	A	B	H
B	X	N	A	B	H	Y

There are also two subsets of the set (H, Y, X, N, A, B), and each one is a group in itself. Such *groups are called subgroups.* (Note that the elements of the subgroup are placed in the order in which they appeared for the subjects on the dial of the machine on which they worked.)

	H	N
H	N	H
N	H	N

	Y	N	B
Y	B	Y	N
N	Y	N	B
B	N	B	Y

The 6-group is interesting because it can be generated in two ways: either from the single generator X, since we have all the elements of the set (H, Y, X, N, A, B) in

X □ X.X=Y, □ X.X.X=H, □ X.X.X.X=B,
X.X.X.X.X=A, □ X.X.X.X.X.X=N;

or from the two elements H and Y, as follows:

HYY=X, □ Y, □ H, □ YY=B, □ HY=A, □ HH=N.

These two methods of generation can be illustrated graphically as

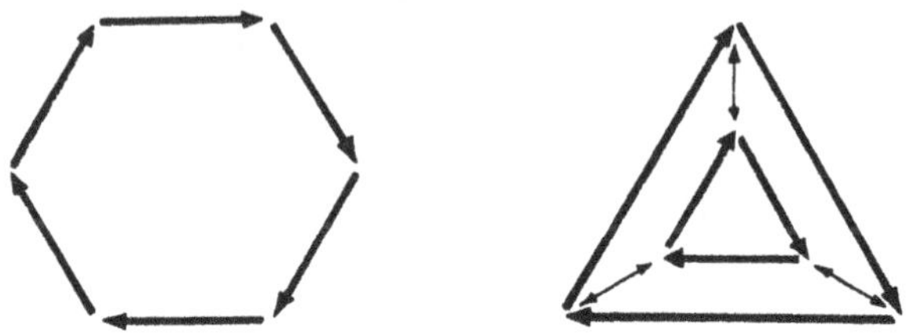

where the first illustrates how every element can be generated from X, and the second illustrates the two-generator situation, where the dark arrow denotes the element Y and the light arrow the element H.

The way in which the 6-group outcome-table is set out above displays the cyclic nature of the structure; we can see that each 'multiplication' by a further X brings the outcome one step to the left. But if the 3-by-2 nature of the structure is to be brought out, we may rearrange the table as follows:

	N	A	B	H	Y	X
N	N	A	B	H	Y	X
A	A	B	N	X	H	Y
B	B	N	A	Y	X	H
H	H	X	Y	N	B	A
Y	Y	H	X	B	A	N
X	X	Y	H	A	N	B

In this ordering we can see the 3-group being 'multiplied' by the 2-group. Every 3-by-3 cell (of which there are four) exhibits the structure of the 3-group, yet the four large cells themselves exhibit the structure of the 2-group. Strictly speaking, only the cells containing {N, A, B} obey the 3-group structure, while the two {H, Y, X} cells are distributed as reflections of the neighbouring {N, A, B} cells. Finally, we can rearrange the table yet once more:

	N	H	B	Y	A	X
N	N	H	B	Y	A	X
H	H	N	Y	B	X	A
B	B	Y	A	X	N	H
Y	Y	B	X	A	H	N
A	A	X	N	H	B	Y
X	X	A	H	N	Y	B

In this ordering, we can see the 2-group being 'multiplied' by the 3-group. Every 2-by-2 cell exhibits the 2-group structure, yet the nine 2-by-2 cells, containing respectively elements of the sets {N, H}, {B, Y}, {A, X}, clearly exhibit the 3-group structure.

Thus, there appear to be at least three ways of organising the data, which from the psychological point of view are very different organisations.

The mathematical group with seven elements

This is represented by a circle with seven points, and correspondingly there are seven moves. One is the neutral move, that is, the no-move or the all-the-way-around move. There are six others: one move, two moves, or three moves clockwise, and one move, two moves, or three moves counter-clockwise. The mathematical group with seven elements is represented by the relationships between these moves. Clearly, this game is also cyclic because every move will be generated by means of one of its members. For example, the clockwise move of one space, or the clockwise move of two spaces, when done a sufficient number of times, will generate all the other elements.

It has already been pointed out that some cyclic groups cannot be generated by every one of their members. For example, the cyclic group of six elements will never be generated if we start with the two clockwise or the two counter-clockwise. If we do, we shall only get three moves: the two counter-clockwise, the two clockwise, and the no-move. We shall never be able to generate the one clockwise or the one counter-clockwise or the half-the-way-around move, simply because six is not a prime number. But any mathematical group in which the number of elements is a prime number can be generated by any one of its members except the neutral element.

Here is the outcome-table for the 7-group:

	Z	Y	X	N	A	B	C
Z	A	B	C	Z	Y	X	N
Y	B	C	Z	Y	X	N	A
X	C	Z	Y	X	N	A	B
N	Z	Y	X	N	A	B	C
A	Y	X	N	A	B	C	X
B	X	N	A	B	C	X	Y
C	N	A	B	C	X	Y	Z

The cyclic group with nine elements

This can obviously be represented by means of a circle with nine points marked along its circumference. There will be a one-move, a two-move, a three-move, and a four-move, clockwise and counter-clockwise, making eight elements, and the ninth is the neutral move. The group can be generated by some of its members, but not by the neutral move or either of the three moves. So this group is also cyclic, as can be deduced from this representation:

	Z	Y	X	W	N	A	B	C	D
Z	A	B	C	D	Z	Y	X	W	N
Y	B	C	D	Z	Y	X	W	N	A
X	C	D	Z	Y	X	W	N	A	B
W	D	Z	Y	X	W	N	A	B	C
N	Z	Y	X	W	N	A	B	C	D
A	Y	X	W	N	A	B	C	D	Z
B	X	W	N	A	B	C	D	Z	Y
C	W	N	A	B	C	D	Z	Y	X
D	N	A	B	C	D	Z	Y	X	W

The direct product 9-group

Let us select three shapes: say, squares, triangles, and circles. Let us make the circle the neutral shape, and the square and the triangle the shapes which will generate the 3-group, that is, the mathematical group with three elements. A square operating on a square will generate a triangle. A triangle operating on a triangle will generate a square. A square and a triangle operating on each other will generate a circle. The circle is the neutral element; and the triangle and square correspond to the clockwise move and the counter-clockwise move or to the numbers which, divided by three, left remainders of one and of two respectively. This, then, defines a 3-group on shapes.

Now let us consider colours. We will select red, orange and yellow and decide that yellow is to be the neutral colour. Then red and red will produce orange, and orange and orange will produce red; and red and orange will produce yellow.

To produce the combined outcome-table (shapes and colours), we draw nine large squares in three rows of three, and in each of these squares we draw three rows of three shapes. In the figure below, it will be seen that the 3-group is repeated in each of the nine large squares by means of the colours, and that in the overall 3-by-3 structure the 3-group operates through the shapes. The combination of these two 3-by-3 effects is known as the direct product of the group of three elements by the group of three elements. (This constituted task 9A in our experiment.)

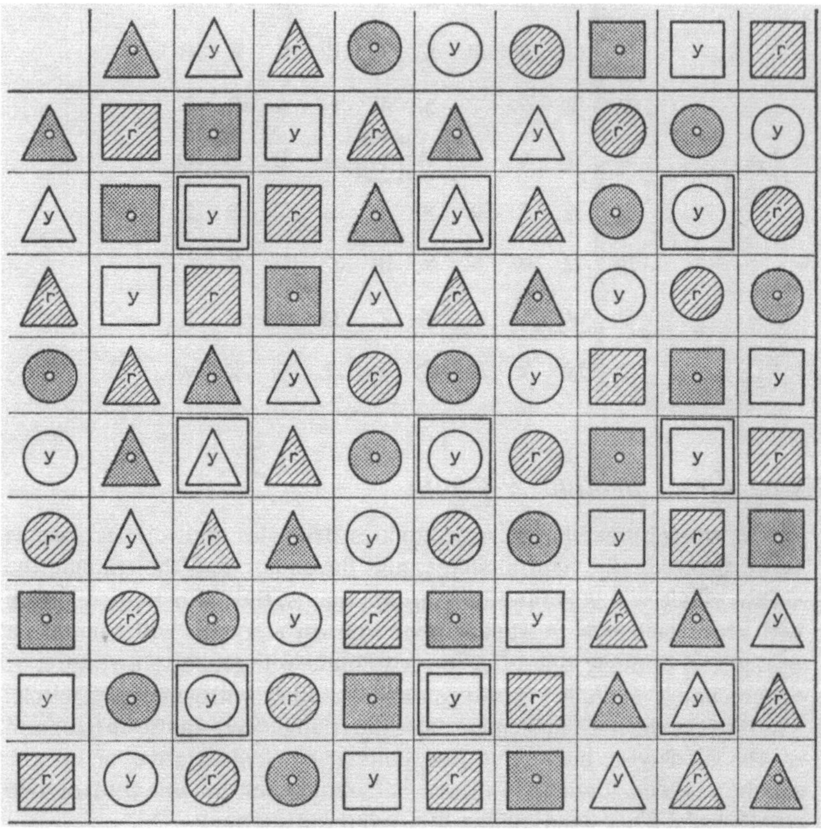

Here we can actually see the 3-group 'multiplied' by the 3-group, as the configuration of the large 3-by-3 cells follows the same rules as the configuration of the elements within each 3-by-3 cell. It can be proved, also, that there is no way of generating all the elements from any single element. The group is therefore not cyclic.

In this schematic diagram of the cyclic 9-group, if →=x, then the elements are x, xx, xxx, xxxx, xxxxx, xxxxxx, xxxxxxx, xxxxxxxx, xxxxxxxxx.

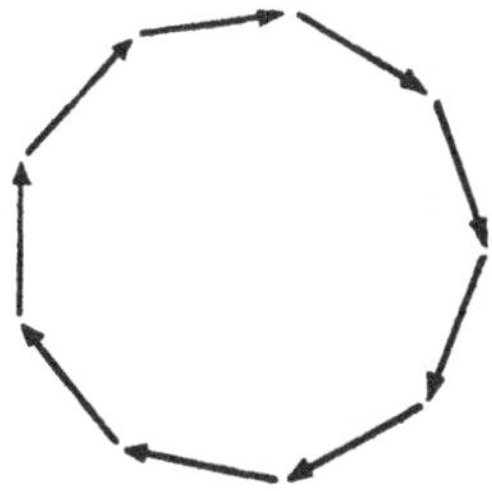

On the other hand, in this 3-by-3 group (or 9A), if →=x, ⇒=y, then the elements are x, xx, y, yy, xy, xyy, yxx, xxyy, xxx. The positions are marked by the successions of the generating moves that need to be done to get there from an arbitrarily chosen 'Home'.

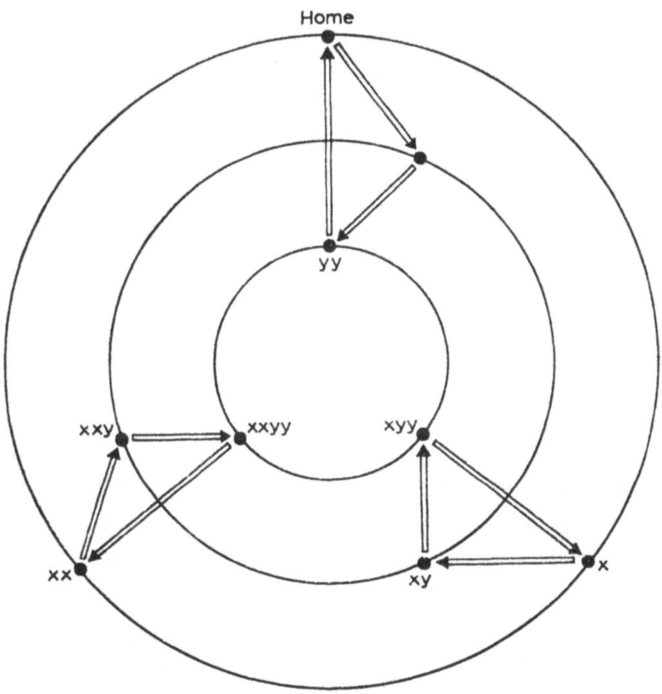

Relationships between the structures used

The mathematical groups just described stand in certain relationships to one another. As one of the purposes of the experiment was to study the effect of this on learning and transfer, something must be said about the nature of these relationships.

Any two sets of objects, neither of which is empty, can stand to each other in one of five relationships. Supposing the sets are a and b, these relationships are as follows:

(1) a is identical with b
(2) a is included in b
(3) b is included in a
(4) a and b are quite disjoint
with no common elements
(5) a and b effectively overlap.

In the case of mathematical groups, disjointness (4), that is, the relationship of complete non-overlapping, is impossible. Since every mathematical group must have a neutral element, this provides an overlap between any two mathematical groups. (There might, of course, be a further overlap, so far as the psychologist is concerned.)

The interest of the identity situation (1) lies in the possibility of determining to what extent subjects are able to detect identity when structures are presented to them in different forms. This is part of the process of abstraction; in fact, it is this identity of structure which is called the abstract property of the structure.

However, in this particular experiment no studies were made on the identity problem. The relationships were either of inclusion or of overlapping.

The obvious cases of overlapping are between the 6-group and the two 9-groups. It is quite clear that the cyclic group of six elements contains the 3-group as a subgroup. Furthermore, both the cyclic group of nine elements and the direct product 9-element group have the 3-group as a subgroup. The 3-group thus provides the overlap. The 6-group is, of course, not included in the 9-group; there is no subgroup in the 9-group which is isomorphic to the 6-group.

There is an overlap between the Klein 4-group and the 6-group, since both these groups contain the 2-group. In fact, the Klein group contains the 2-group three times over. In our representation, 'the neutral' with 'changing a' is one 2-group; 'the neutral' with 'changing b' is another 2-group; and 'the neutral' with 'changing a and b' is another 2-group. In the group of six elements, the 'all-the-way-around' and 'half-way-around' form the 2-group. The 2-group is not a subgroup of any of the other groups studied.

These are only the most obvious overlappings and inclusions. In the case of 9A, that is, the direct product of the 3-group by itself, there is a more subtle inclusion. In this structure the group is mirrored in itself as many times as the subgroup has elements, as will be seen in the diagram on page 32. The arrangement of the nine major squares in the matrix is mirrored in the arrangement of the elements that compose the squares. This sort of inclusion is a more powerful kind of inclusion than the mere inclusion of a structure as a subgroup. Exactly the same applied to the Klein group which is the product of the 2-group by the 2-group. One might usefully discuss the differences and similarities that result from more powerful and subtle inclusions of this kind, compared to the less powerful and more obvious inclusion of a subgroup in a group.

One way to make these relationships of inclusion and identity clear is to think of mappings between the various structures. Let us take, for example, the 6-group discussed before, with the set of elements

(N, H, B, Y, A, X).

The embodiment in terms of 'third of a turn', 'sixth of a turn', 'half turn' and 'no turn' could be matched against the set of symbols above (together with the accompanying rule structure, exemplified in the outcome-table), and the question asked: 'Which corresponds to which?' In this case we should find the correspondence:

N→no turn, H→half turn, B→third of a turn clockwise, Y→sixth of a turn counter-clockwise, A→third of a turn counter-clockwise, X→sixth of a turn clockwise.

The correspondence works both ways; the results of the binary operations in one 'game' will correspond to the results of the corresponding elements in the 'other game'. So we have established what in mathematics is known as an *isomorphism* between the two structures, which means that, structurally speaking, there is nothing to choose between the two descriptions.

We might wish to emphasise the 'direct product' aspect of a structure, in which case we need to make a correspondence between a structure and one of its sub-structures. To show that we have an 'overall 2-group', we can make the correspondence:

N→N, A→N, B→N, H→H, Y→H, X→H

This only works one way, but the translated relationships remain true. AY=H will translate into NH=H, which is true. (The reader should verify that this is so in all cases.)

If we wished to emphasise the overall 3-group, we should find:

$$N \to N,\ H \to N,\ B \to B,\ Y \to B,\ A \to A,\ X \to A$$

This again is a one-way transformation, but preserves the truth of the translated, transformed statements. YX=N will translate into BA=N, and so on. This is known as a *homomorphism.*

An isomorphism is the construction of a bridge between two structures that are structurally similar. A homomorphism is a one-way street leading from a structure to a 'smaller' structure. In effect, it establishes a one-to-many correspondence, whereas an isomorphism establishes a one-to-one correspondence.

A homomorphism is present where there is an overlap. For example, the 6-group and the 4-group overlap in the 2-group. We can establish three homomorphisms, one from the 6-group to the 2-group and one from each of the 4-groups to the 2-group.

Let the 2-group be represented by the set of elements (e a), where e e=e, a a=a, a e=a, a a=e, then the homomorphisms are as follows:

N to e, A to e, B to e, H to a, Y to a, X to a
(from 6-group to 2-group)
(1) to a, (2) to a, (3) to e, (4) to e
(from Klein group to 2-group)
(1) to a, (2) to e, (3) to a, (4) to e
(from cyclic 4-group to 2-group)

Isomorphisms and homomorphisms have not been directly used as learning material. They are only discussed here so as to make clear some of the relationships which are present in the stimulus material handled by the subjects and relevant to the discussion of their responses.

Generation of structures by rules

Amongst the stimulus material there are the following cyclic groups:

3-group, 5-group, 6-group, 7-group, 9-group.

Each of these is generated by a single element. The only difference between them is in the number of times this generating element has to be combined with itself before the neutral element is obtained. If a is the generating element, for the 3-group we stipulate that

a.a.a=neutral element

or using the conventional shorter 'power' notation,

$a^3=e$ (where e stands for the neutral)

Similarly, $a^5=e$ gives us the rule of generation of the cyclic 5-group. In fact, the 'exponent' in this determination-rule indicates which cyclic group we are dealing with.

When we come to the 6-group, the situation is more complicated since it is possible to generate the group in two ways. If a and b are the generators, we can say that

$$a^2=e,\ b^3=e.$$

But this does not give us the relationship between a and b; and unless we give this relationship, it would be possible to generate an infinite number of elements out of the two rules. For example,

$$a\,b\,b\,a\,b\,b\,a\,b\,a\,b\,a\,b\,b$$

would certainly be an element. But if we add the requirement that

$$a\,b=b\,a$$

then we can 'prove' that the longwinded element above is 'the same element as' $a\,b\,b$. This is done by successive interchanges of a's and b's, and by the omission of strings such as $b\,b\,b$ or $a\,a$, which by the first two rules are equivalent to e, the neutral element. In this 'proof', we rely on the associativity of the binary operation. If the operation were not associative, the longwinded element would have no meaning unless we inserted brackets to show in what way the elements are associated. So, we can replace the generation rule

$$x^6=e,$$

by the group of generation rules

$$a^2=e,\ b^3=e,\ a\,b=b\,a,$$

which will generate the same structure. This is why passing from $x^5=e$ to $x^6=e$ is not such a simple matter as passing from $x^5=e$ to $x^7=e$, where no such complications about alternative generation of the structure occurs.

Now, the Klein group is generated by

$$a^2=e,\ b^2=e,\ a\,b=b\,a.$$

If we alter the exponent in b^2 to b^3, we obtain the 6-group as a *generalisation* of the Klein group, looked at from the point of view of 2-element generation. Psychologically speaking, it is no doubt irrelevant that the Klein group also cannot be generated from one element.

If we pass on to the 3-by-3 group, we have another generalisation to do, namely we must change a^2 into a^3 as well as change b^2 into b^3.

So there are three 2-element-generation generalisations that we can make.

(1) $a^2=e,\ b^2=e,\ a\,b=b\,a$ generalises into
$a^2=e,\ b^3=e,\ a\,b=b\,a$ where b^2 changes to b^3
(2) $a^2=e,\ b^3=e,\ a\,b=b\,a$ generalises into
$a^3=e,\ b^3=e,\ a\,b=b\,a$ where a^2 changes to a^3
(3) $a^2=e,\ b^2=e,\ a\,b=b\,a$ generalises into
$a^3=e,\ b^3=e,\ a\,b=b\,a$ where a^2 changes to a^3
b^2 changes to b^3

In the first case we generalise from the Klein group to the 6-group; in the second, from the 6-group to the 3-by-3 group; and in the third, from the Klein group to the 3-by-3 group.

It could be argued that the third kind of generalisation is easier than the other two, as the value of the two exponents is stepped up by the same amount, so that the 'feel' of the structure remains very similar, as it does when we generalise from

$$x^5=e \text{ to } x^7=e$$

In both cases the generalisation makes the structure 'similar but bigger', whereas in the case of (1) and (2) there is something 'lopsided' about the generalisation.

Note that, with the Klein group, the requirement of commutativity, i.e. $a\,b=b\,a$, can also be stated as $a\,b\,a\,b=e$; but not in the other cases. In fact, if we replace

$$a^2=e,\ b^3=e,\ a\,b=b\,a$$

by

$$a^2=e,\ b^3=e,\ a\,b\,a\,b=e$$

we shall no longer have the properties of the cyclic 6-group but those of the dihedral 6-group, which is non-commutative.

This latter group is isomorphic to the set of rotations and reflections that can be performed on an equilateral triangle, which brings it back to its original *space* but not necessarily to its original position. It is thus possible to generalise on yet another 'front', by changing the third condition. This was not included in the series of experiments described in this book, but raises interesting questions. For example,

$$a^3=e,\ b^3=e,\ a\,b\,a\,b=e$$

will produce all the rotations of a regular tetrahedron, which bring it back to occupy the same space as before, but not necessarily the same position. How the study of such geometrical facts connects with the study of structure relationships of a recursive character will form part of our further studies.

3

The experimental design and the performance measures used

In this chapter we shall indicate how the mathematical groups described in the previous chapter were embodied in an electrical machine so that they could be presented as a problem-solving task. We shall also explain how, by giving each subject in the experiment a series of four tasks to be solved on succeeding days, we were able to study some of the transfer effects of the learning of one task upon others. Finally, we shall list the performance measures used to assess excellence of performance and the indices devised to make possible a quantitative description of the types of performance shown by our subjects.

Techniques used

In the last round of experiments described in *Thinking in Structures* most of the structures studied were relatively simple. They mostly comprised structures with two elements and four elements, though some limited studies were done in structures with more than four elements. As a result, it was possible to make records of subjects' performances by hand and study the relationships involved in fairly conventional ways. However, as soon as one increases the complexity of the task beyond this level it becomes necessary to mechanise the task in some way. It was clearly impossible to obtain a sufficient number of trained experimenters to administer large numbers of tasks of higher and higher complexity, keep the experimental design satisfactory and maintain the control necessary for a scientifically valid inquiry. An electrical machine was therefore constructed which recorded the responses and predictions of the subject as he made them, and the output of the machine was automatically punched on to cards in a form which could be fed immediately into a computer. This method of recording responses had one very important advantage in analysing the results of the experiment. In spite of the complexities of strategy and hypothesis used by the subjects, and the detailed analysis which was therefore necessary, it was possible, with the data recorded on IBM punch cards, to subject it to many complex questions in a limited amount of time.

The electrical machine which performs the duties of the experimenter is in effect very simple. It consists of three panels: the 'State', 'Play' and 'Predict' panels (see diagram, p. 42). There are ten possible windows in each panel, all dimly illuminated so that the symbols can easily be discriminated. The symbol representing the actual state of the machine at any time is brightly lit, in the 'State' panel; so also is the symbol the subject wishes to play, in the 'Play' panel, and the symbol that is his prediction of the next state of the machine, in the 'Predict' panel. The windows can be covered by different transparencies and thus the symbols can be varied at will; but for any given task the same symbols are used for all subjects in the same positions in each of the three panels. In the central upper display panel, the 'State' panel, the brightly illuminated window is controlled by the machine; but the two lower panels, the 'Play' and 'Predict' panels, have switches which can be operated by the subject. The subject is able to manipulate the 'Play' switch and thus move the operator, i.e. the bright light, to any window. Similarly, the 'Predict' switch can be turned by the subject to indicate his prediction. The subject then presses the 'GO' button in order to activate the machine. This causes the machine to put into effect the operation which is the result of the present state in conjunction with the operator illuminated on the 'Play' panel; the next state of the machine depends only on these two variables. If the prediction is correct a green light comes on; if incorrect a red light comes on. But, quite apart from this, the subject is aware whether he is correct or incorrect because the next state of the machine becomes clearly visible on the 'State' panel, after the 'GO' button has been pressed.

To facilitate the association of the state of the machine and the operator part of the machine, lines were drawn around these parts to draw the attention of the subject to the relationship between the two. (A photograph of the machine is shown facing page 48, at the end of this chapter.)

The machine was capable of two kinds of operation, referred to as the A Operation and the B Operation. The A Operation has just been described. In the B Operation, the subject did not have the choice of operating, but only the choice of predicting. The B Operation meant that the machine automatically took the subject through all the possible

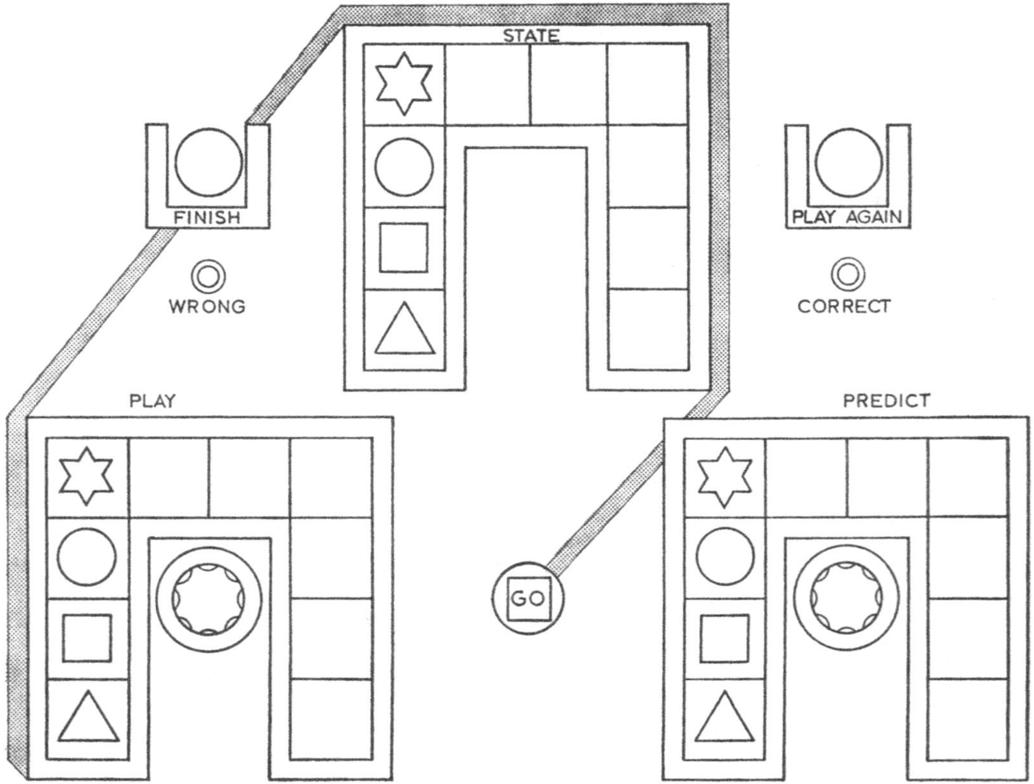
STATE
FINISH
WRONG
PLAY AGAIN
CORRECT
PLAY
PREDICT
GO

combinations of states and operators and asked the subject to respond with the appropriate prediction. In other words, in the B Operation the subject only predicted, whilst in the A Operation he operated and predicted. After a predetermined number of trials, each subject was given the B Operation at the end of the session.

Clearly, the tasks could be varied enormously. One merely had to decide what combination of states and operators would result in what further states. It was possible to programme any desired combinations into the machine. This was done on a programming square at the back of the machine (shown in the photograph facing page 49), and the programme was adjusted before each subject came in. Some of the tasks involved only three states and the corresponding operators, others, four states and the corresponding operators, and so on. The largest number of states and corresponding operators used was nine. The only number that was not used was eight states and eight operators. That is, 3-, 4-, 5-, 6-, 7- and 9-element situations were all used at various times.

Whilst mathematical groups were selected as the most suitable structures for this series of experiments, it is by no means necessary to restrict oneself to these. The closed structure of a group does, however, make it particularly suitable for experimenting and probably also promotes ease in learning as well. However that may be, all the structures used in these experiments were mathematical groups. In Chapter 2 we have described in detail the groups that were used, namely (A) the 3-group, (B) the Klein group, which is a mathematical group with four elements, (C) the 5-group, (D) the cyclic 6-group, (E) the 7-group, (F) the cyclic 9-group, (G) the 9-group which is a direct product of the 3-group by itself. The outcomes, that is, the states which were the consequences of the previous states and the operators selected by the subjects, were fully determined by these group structures, of course. There was no question of one outcome being more probable than another outcome. Every outcome was either certain or impossible.

Administration of the task

Every effort was made to ensure that each subject fully understood what was required of him before the session began. We do not mean that we attempted to describe in detail the nature of the problem to be solved since this was in fact one of the things we were studying. But we made every effort to put each subject at his ease and to reassure him that there was no 'catch' in what he was being asked to do, as subjects are often inclined to feel when they take part in psychological experiments. The experimenter explained to the subject that he was taking part in an experiment aimed at studying how people set about thinking in certain situations. With adult subjects, a standard instruction sheet was read to them and they were asked to follow the directions on the machine in front of them. They were also allowed to ask questions which they felt would clarify for them exactly what they were to do. The instruction sheet read as follows:

You are going to play a game against this machine. The top part here (pointing) is the machine. This part here on the left (pointing) is *you*.

The machine can at any time be in one of four *states*. You can tell in which state the machine is, by the light that is on. At the moment the machine is in the *red circle state*. During the game, the machine will go through a number of different states, that is, the light will go on in different windows, but of course in only one window at a time.

You have four different 'plays' on *your* part. These are shown by means of the same pictures as you see on the machine (pointing out the identity of the symbols). This is like this one, this is like this one, this is like this one, and this is like this one.

The state which is going to come up next in the machine will depend on (1) what you play, *and* (2) on the state in which the machine is already. From knowing in which state the machine is, and from knowing what you play, it is possible to know beforehand what state is going to come up next in the machine, *if you know the rules of the machine*. When you know these, you have beaten the machine.

To make the next state come up, you have to press the 'GO' button. Press the button well in and then let go. You will then, after a few seconds, notice a new state coming up in the machine.

The way to beat the machine is to know beforehand what it is going to do next. Before you press the 'GO' button, you should tell the machine what state is coming up next by turning this knob (pointing to the knob on the right), and putting the light in the picture which is the same picture as the one that you think is going to come up. For example, if you think that a yellow circle is going to come up next, then you turn this knob until the light comes into the yellow circle. Then you press the 'GO' button, and you will soon see if you were right or wrong. If the machine goes into the state that you thought of, a green light will go on here. If it goes into some other state, then a red light will go on here.

When you decide what you *think* the machine is going to do next, do not forget to tell the machine this by turning the 'predictor knob' (pointing) to the picture which you think is going to come up in the machine, and say to yourself aloud 'red circle against red circle will give me yellow circle' for example, or whatever it is that you think is going to happen. It is good to say these predictions aloud, because then you will still remember which state you played against, even though this state is now no longer on the machine because you have pressed the 'GO' button.

Only use the first four pictures here on the left. This game only uses these. One of these four pictures will always come up during this game, so do not predict any other states but one of these four.

Your job is to find out what the machine will do when you play any of your pictures against any of the machine's pictures. Remember, you will need to know what *anything* against *anything* will produce before you can say that you have beaten the machine.

This is not a test to see how clever you are, nor indeed is it a test at all. We are interested in how people think things out, and the reason you are doing this is to give us ideas about *how* you set about beating the machine. In the end you will have a chance to show what you have found out about the machine.

Are you quite clear about what the whole thing is about? If you are not, you can ask any questions now. Once you have started, we don't want you to ask any questions.

The subjects were then given a résumé of the task in more concrete terms. The gist of what the experimenter added was as follows:

All you have to do is to play—and by play I mean move the light to one of the symbols, like this (demonstrate)—one of the symbols against or with the symbol showing in the top panel (point to it)—and then try to predict what you think the answer or result of the combination of these two (pointing to them) will be. You then move the light to that symbol (pointing to prediction panel) and press the 'GO' button like this (press button). (The experimenter always started with red circle + red circle→red circle—which was incorrect, since yellow circle came up in state panel.)

You can see that my prediction was wrong because the red light 'your prediction was wrong' is lit up, and also the correct answer, which is now showing on the state panel, is not the same as the one you predicted. You have to remember that two (point to both) red circles, which is what you started with—you remember you had a red circle in the state panel (pointing to it)—make a yellow circle (pointing to it). You have to remember what you had in the state panel because as soon as you press the 'GO' button it will disappear and you will get the answer to the previous combination.

All you have to do, then, is to play any symbol on this panel (pointing to play panel) with the one that is showing at the top, and try to predict the result. At first you will just be guessing, but you will have to try and find ways of successfully predicting the different combinations because later on you will be asked some questions and the machine will test you to see how much you know. Any questions?

If for any reason the subject still seemed unclear about any part of the instructions or the way the machine worked, he was allowed to have a 'go' and at the same time he was encouraged to explain what he thought he was doing as he went along to the experimenter.

The subjects were not told how many 'goes' they would have on any task, but if they specifically asked how many, they were told that they would have 'quite a lot' and that the bell would ring when they had had their quota.

In the case of the children it was essential to simplify the instructions and to do everything possible to ensure that they understood what was required of them. As a result of experience with the first few subjects, it was found that by reading the following instructions to them, slowly, and by illustrating each point, it was possible in most cases to be reasonably certain that they understood the task.

> This is a game which you are going to play with the machine. You have to try and beat the machine by finding out what it is going to do next. These panels are all exactly the same—they have the same four pictures (go through each one). This panel is the machine. This panel is *your* panel—you have to 'play' one of your pictures with the machine's picture and then predict (that means, say what you think will happen) what the result of playing those two together will be. You predict, or tell the machine, what you think the answer will be, by turning this knob to the one you think is correct. When you have done this you press the 'GO' button.

The experimenter then demonstrated first with two red circles→red circle to show that this was wrong, and then showed where the right answer comes up on the machine and emphasised that the subject must remember what was there before, i.e. red circle+red circle→yellow circle. The experimenter then gave one correct demonstration. She then let the subject have one 'go' and quickly repeated the sequence of action, emphasising that the subject must wait till the 'GO' button came out, and must not move the light any further round than four. The experimenter further told the subject that he would just have to guess to begin with, but emphasised that he must try and learn what *everything* with *everything* would make because she would ask him some questions afterwards and the machine would give him a test to see how much he knew. As an additional safeguard the experimenter, before starting the experiment, also asked each child to explain to her what it was that he was required to do.

After completing a task the experimenter asked the subject a number of questions and recorded their answers. The questions were:

(1) What does this game remind you of?

If there was no response, then:

(1a) Does it remind you of anything you have done at school, or at University (the latter only if applicable)? Or of things you do every day?

(2) Try to describe the rules of the game in as simple a way as you can.

If there was no response, or if the subject appeared to think that he had merely learned to remember all the combinations, the experimenter tried to elicit further responses by questions such as:

'Isn't there some way in which the game hangs together?' *or*
'Tell me something about the yellow circle, or any of the others.'

The experimenter tried to note down as fully as possible the subject's responses to such questioning. While the subject was responding, the experimenter did not interrupt or prompt, but merely took notes. If there was a negative response to the question

'Are there any other ways in which you could describe the game or parts of the game?'

the experimenter went on to the next part:

(3) 'Equations' questions (see pages 48–51). These were given with each programme. If the subject corrected himself, the experimenter noted this down, whether the corrections were correct or incorrect.

(4) The experimenter asked the following further questions: 'If you change around the "Play" and the "State" against which you play, do you get the same next state or do you get a different one? For example, is a red circle against a yellow triangle going to give the same next state as a yellow triangle against a red circle?'

If the question seemed unclear, it was elucidated by further examples. The experimenter tried to elicit the response before the subject had a chance to test his hypothesis. Having elicited a response, then if the subject wished to test it, he was allowed to do so. Any consequent change of opinion was recorded.

EQUATIONS TO BE SOLVED IN EACH TASK

We have several times referred to the equations which were presented to subjects at the completion of the A Operation. They were presented in the form: 'What would you play with a yellow frame to get a yellow frame?' This was a way of presenting, in the terms of the symbols used in the machine, an equation of the form: 'Where Ax=B what is the value of x?' We give below in summary form the equations presented after each group had been played on the machine. (The reader is reminded that symbols such as A and B were not, of course, given to the subjects, but are used below for clarity of presentation.)

Four game

	A	B	C	D
A	D	C	B	A
B	C	D	A	B
C	B	A	D	C
D	A	B	C	D

Equations given for solutions:

Ax=A; Bx=B; Dx=B; Dx=C; Dx=D;
Ax=D; Bx=D; Cx=D; Cx=A; Bx=C;
Ax=B.

Three game

	A	B	C
A	C	A	B
B	A	B	C
C	B	C	A

Equations given for solutions:

Ax=A; Cx=C; Bx=B; Ax=C; Cx=A;
Bx=A; Bx=C; Cx=B; Ax=B.

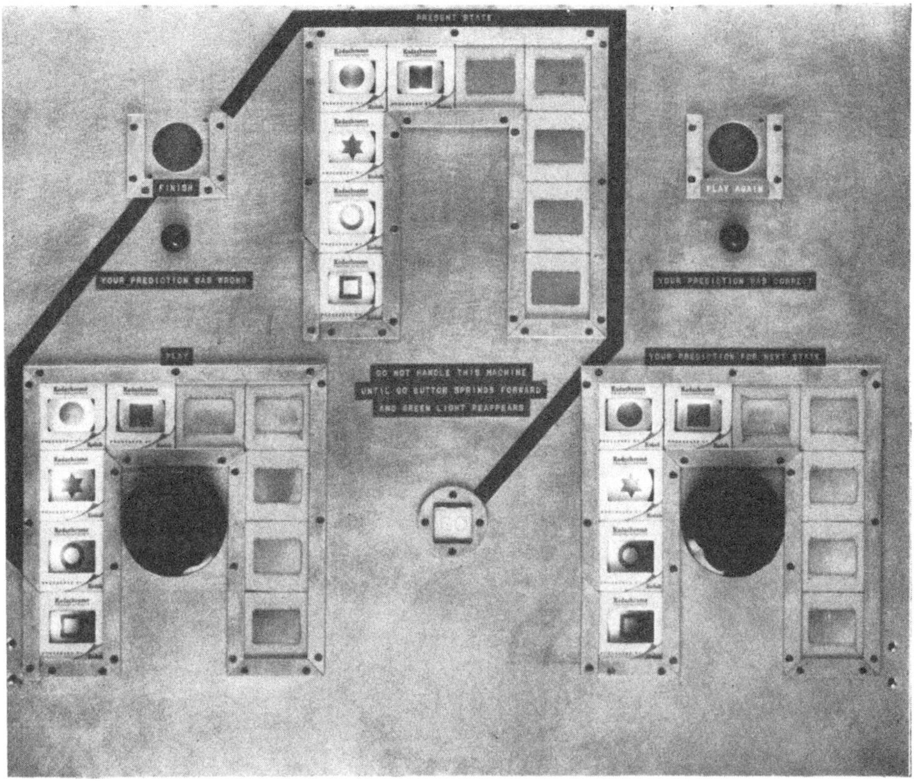

Front of machine

Programme square in back of machine

Five game

	A	B	C	D	E
A	D	E	A	B	C
B	E	A	B	C	D
C	A	B	C	D	E
D	B	C	D	E	A
E	C	D	E	A	B

Equations given for solutions:

Ax=A; Dx=D; Cx=B; Cx=E; Cx=C;
Bx=A; Dx=E; Ax=D; Bx=D; Ex=A.

Seven game

	A	B	C	D	E	F	G
A	E	F	G	A	B	C	D
B	F	G	A	B	C	D	E
C	G	A	B	C	D	E	F
D	A	B	C	D	E	F	G
E	B	C	D	E	F	G	A
F	C	D	E	F	G	A	B
G	D	E	F	G	A	B	C

Equations given for solutions:

Ax=A; Ex=E; Dx=B; Dx=G; Dx=D;
Bx=G; Cx=B; Ax=E; Gx=C; Gx=B;
Bx=A; Ex=G.

Six game

	A	B	C	D	E	F
A	D	E	F	A	B	C
B	E	F	A	B	C	D
C	F	A	B	C	D	E
D	A	B	C	D	E	F
E	B	C	D	E	F	A
F	C	D	E	F	A	B

Equations given for solutions:

Bx=B; Ex=E; Dx=C; Dx=F; Dx=D; Cx=D;
Fx=D; Ax=D; Cx=E; Ex=C; Cx=A; Ax=B.

Nine game

	A	B	C	D	E	F	G	H	I
A	F	G	H	I	A	B	C	D	E
B	G	H	I	A	B	C	D	E	F
C	H	I	A	B	C	D	E	F	G
D	I	A	B	C	D	E	F	G	H
E	A	B	C	D	E	F	G	H	I
F	B	C	D	E	F	G	H	I	A
G	C	D	E	F	G	H	I	A	B
H	D	E	F	G	H	I	A	B	C
I	E	F	G	H	I	A	B	C	D

Equations given for solutions:

Bx=B; Ix=I; Ex=C; Ex=F; Ex=E; Cx=A;
Hx=B; Fx=G; Gx=C; Dx=I; Cx=B; Fx=H.

Nine A game

	A	B	C	D	E	F	G	H	I
A	I	G	H	C	A	B	F	D	E
B	G	H	I	A	B	C	D	E	F
C	H	I	G	B	C	A	E	F	D
D	C	A	B	F	D	E	I	G	H
E	A	B	C	D	E	F	G	H	I
F	B	C	A	E	F	D	H	I	G
G	F	D	E	I	G	H	C	A	B
H	D	E	F	G	H	I	A	B	C
I	E	F	D	H	I	G	B	C	A

Equations given for solutions:

Dx=D; Ix=I; Bx=B; Ex=H; Ex=C; Ex=F;
Ax=I; Dx=F; Ix=A; Gx=A; Cx=G; Gx=F.

Subject characteristics

Two groups of subjects took part in the experiments, one of adults and the other of children. The adults were university students enrolled in a first-year course in psychology as part of a general arts course. One of the requirements of the psychology course was that each student should take part in four hours of experimenting to increase his acquaintance with the method and content of psychology, and their participation in this experiment was in fulfilment of this requirement. The children who took part were from Cowandilla Demonstration School, South Australia. Their average age was eleven years. IQs based on group-administered tests were available for eighteen of the children and ranged from 96 to 132 with a mean of 114·06 and standard deviation of 10·22. There were approximately equal numbers of males and females in both the adult and children groups. It is our opinion that the IQs of the university students did not differ substantially from those of the children.

The experimental design

The experiments were designed to investigate: (a) the effects of various group structures upon the learning of the structures; and (b) the effect of learning one structure upon the learning of other structures which were related to the earlier ones in clearly specifiable and definable ways. In addition, the design was so constructed that the effects of overlap and of embeddedness would be comparable with the effects of recursion, whether in the form of generalisation or of particularisation. Every subject started with the Klein group which, as a result of earlier experiments, was thought to be the easiest for beginners. This stage was regarded principally as practice in handling the machine and in learning to think in terms of the kind of situation they were going to be confronted with in the remainder of the experiment. Even so, some tentative conclusions will be drawn from the relationships between the learning of this group and the successive groups that were learned afterwards. Table 3.1, which sets out the experimental design, indicates the different courses followed by various groups of subjects. The same pattern was followed for both adults and children. (From now on, the cyclic 9-group will be referred to as '9', and the 9 direct-product 3-by-3 group as '9A', for simplicity.)

Number of subjects	*Day 1*	*Day 2*	*Day 3*	*Day 4*
10	Klein 4	3	5	7
10	Klein 4	5	3	7
10	Klein 4	3	6	9
10	Klein 4	6	3	9
10	Klein 4	3	6	9A (3 × 3)
10	Klein 4	6	3	9A (3 × 3)

TABLE 3.1

In the first part of the design, although there was a certain amount of generalisation, for example from 3 to 6, there was also embeddedness, since the 3-group is included once as a subgroup of the 6-group. Of course, it is also a generalisation of the 3-group situation, but not as easy a generalisation as the 5-group is of the 3-group. The reason for this is that the 6-group has an even number of elements, whereas the 5-group and the 3-group have an odd number. So, in passing from the 3-group to the 5-group, if the element in the middle is regarded as the neutral, one on each side of the neutral would be the 3-group and two on each side of the neutral would be the 5-group. This is naturally impossible in the case of the 6-group. Thus, one easy form of generalisation from 3 to 5 is not applicable to 3 to 6. It was hypothesised that the embeddedness relationship between 3 and 6 would be likely to contribute more to the learning of these two groups than to the learning of the 3-group and the 5-group.

In passing from the 6-group to the 9-group, there is a further act of generalisation, and also an overlap. The overlap between the 6-group and 9-group is naturally the 3-group, which is a subgroup of both groups. Thus passing from 6 to 9 involves coping with the generalisation situation as well as with the overlap situation. On the other hand, passing from the 6-group to the 9A-group does not involve any generalisation, but involves a great deal of overlap; the 3-group is included in the 9A-group four times. In the 6-group it occurs only once. There is, therefore, an overlap four times over between the 6-group and the 9A-group. Any transfer effects from 6 to 9A are thus likely to be due to overlapping. On the other hand, any transfer effects from 3 to 5 and 5 to 7 can only be due to the generalisation relationship, as there are no inclusion relationships there.

It should be stressed that the order of presentation of the 3 and 6, as well as of the 3 and 5, was controlled. Again, each of these was followed by a 9 or a 9A or a 7, to be the counterbalancing part of the design. It was found in the first round of the experiments that, in some cases, the subjects who started with the more complex task did rather better in total performance than the others. This was particularly so with the children, although even with the adults a certain amount of generalisation was noticeable in some categories. Clearly, this was something that needed further investigation, to see how far one could push the degree of complexity before it was too complex to serve as a starting-point. In the first round of experiments, only the 2-group and the 4-group were used; the 4-group was apparently not much more complex than the 2-group, and this might have proved to be the optimum complexity. However, we were able to increase the initial complexity gradually by trying 5 preceded by 3 as well as 3 preceded by 5, and 6 preceded by 3 as well as 3 preceded by 6, both with children and adults.

There was also a marked effect attributable to the 'internal symmetry' of the structures that were presented. This effect was more marked with the children than with the adults. Symmetry was defined as the number of automorphisms, that is, self-mappings of the structure on to itself, which left the structure essentially unaltered in all but name. In this experiment, the 9A-group has far more automorphisms than the 9-group. It might well be expected that the relationships between the 9A-group and the 9-group would be similar to those between the Klein group and the cyclic group with four elements. The measures of symmetry in the actual playing of the game will be explained when the scoring categories are given.

The dependent variables

Two distinct kinds of measure were used, those that measured the degree of success or failure of a subject and those that assessed the way in which the subjects had set about tackling the tasks. The first category we shall call '*scores*', and the second category '*indices*'.

Let us consider the three scores used first of all.

(a) *The A Operation score*

In the first phase, each day each subject played a game against the machine for a predetermined number of 'turns'. In the course of this, some of his predictions were correct and some incorrect. The A Operation score is the total number of incorrect predictions during this part of the experiment.

(b) *The Equation score*

At the end of the A Operation, the subject was asked a series of questions (see pages 48–51). These questions were mathematical equations expressed in ordinary language instead of in mathematical symbols (which seemed to frighten many people). The score achieved by a subject on these equations should give a measure of his degree of *understanding* of the overall structure of the task. The presentation of equations in this form required him to examine his cognitive map or schematic organisation of what he had learned about it. This self-examination demands a greater degree of understanding than would be involved in merely recalling by rote a number of combinations of stimulus, response and outcome.

In computing the equation score, we gave two points if the equation was correctly solved, and one point if the solution was half-correct. It was also necessary to apply a correction factor to the equation scores, to allow for the number of equations a subject might get right by chance. Consider the situation where an experimental subject is asked N questions, each with p alternative answers. Let us assume that he answers all the questions, sometimes knowing the answers and sometimes merely guessing. Even if his guesses are completely random, some will by chance be right. If the total number of right answers he gives is R, we may take this as made up of x (the number of answers he knows) plus the number he has guessed right by chance. Our estimate of x will be the best number to take as the measure of his ability to answer correctly (i.e. his score).

If x is the number of answers given rightly because the subject knows the answer, $(N-x)$ is the number of times he is merely guessing, and $(N-x)/p$ is the expected number of such answers to be right by chance:

Then $R=x+(N-x)/p$

so $x-x/p=R-N/p$

and $px-x=Rp-N$

and $x=(Rp-N)/(p-1)$ which is the required corrected score. If he had got all right ($R=N$), the formula would reduce to $x=R$. (That is to say, the direct score needs no correction.)

If he was merely guessing throughout, $x=O$ and $R=N/p$. If he partly knows and partly guesses, x lies somewhere between R and $R-N/p$, and the formula gives the best estimate of its value. It requires a slight modification if we cannot assume that the subject gives an answer to every question. For subjects who occasionally said 'Don't know' the following alternative method of computation was used:

If a subject answers only n of the N questions, the number expected right by chance is $(n-x)/p$ and $x=(Rp-n)/(p-1)$.

In such cases, it is essential to use this formula, since to take R as the score will penalise those subjects who refuse to guess what they don't know. They will be unfairly penalised also by the deduction of N/p from all scores.

(c) *The B Operation score*

When a subject had completed the A Operation phase and answered the equations questions, he was once again asked to make predictions on the machine. This time, both the state of the machine and the play were given to the subject, and he simply had to predict the next state. For each task all the possible combinations of state and play were systematically explored. For the 3-group there were nine combinations; for the 4-group, sixteen; for the 5-group, twenty-five; for the 6-group, thirty-six; for the 7-group, forty-nine; and for the 9- and 9A-groups, eighty-one.

Here again it is necessary to make corrections for chance performance and the same correction formula was used.

We turn now to the second category of measures which we have called 'indices'.

(a) *Position index*

For any particular combination of state with operator, there will be a last time when the subject makes an error. If every play is given a serial number, then the serial number of the play on which the last wrong prediction was made is the position index for that combination. From these indices, it is possible to see at what point of the game each combination has been learned or conditioned. In order to obtain the last error on a certain *set* of combinations, the highest index for any individual member of this set must be taken.

(b) *Instance index*

The instance index is the number of times a certain combination has been played, up to and including the last time it was wrongly predicted. This gives, in a sense, the history of the learning of that particular combination. After the last error, of course, it must be assumed that this combination has been learned. This may not be strictly true since the subject may simply not choose to try the combination again. It thus remains a possibility that, if he had tried it again, he would have made an error.

(c) *Frequency index*

This is the number of times certain combinations were selected by the subject, during the whole of the A Operation phase. In order to evaluate the kind of learning that took place, it will sometimes be necessary to compare the frequency with which the combination was selected by a subject, the position in the game where it was first learned, and the number of times it had to be selected in order to be learned. In other words, the relationship between position index, instance index and frequency index will be important. The instance indices are an extension of the scores that we called extrapolation scores in the last round of experiments. It will be remembered that in the last round, the 4-group followed the 2-group, and the neutral element and the alternator occurred in both the 2-group and the 4-group. In these circumstances it was possible, for subjects without any additional evidence from the 4-group, to predict correctly the effect in the four game of operators that were not in the two game. The extrapolation index was therefore the instance index of the operator over any and every state. It is in this sense that the instance indices are simply extensions of the extrapolation scores.

Instance indices were calculated for each column and for each row as well as for the diagonal, so that it is possible to see immediately how many times a certain operator had to be used before it was used without error. Also, we can see how many times a certain state was played against until it was played against without error, and how many times an operator was played against its own state without error. These questions are answered by looking in the columns, rows and diagonals of the instance matrices (see Appendix facing page 58).

Another kind of extrapolation index is derived as follows. A subject may possibly have failed to try certain combinations during the A Operation, that is, during the time when he was allowed to select his own operators; then, in the B Operation, he might, by extrapolation or generalisation, obtain a correct response to one of these combinations in spite of the fact that he had never actually tried it. The number of these correct predictions divided by the total number of combinations not tried in the A Operation, expressed as a percentage, will give an extrapolation score.

Another type of extrapolation score would occur with a subject given a task which was an extension of a previous task, for example the 5-group after the 3-group. In this case he might correctly predict what would be the outcome for some combinations of the 5-group which had never occurred in the 3-group because it did not form part of the 3-group. To obtain an extrapolation index of this kind, we find the total number of combinations on which no errors were made, and divide these by the total number of new combinations that distinguish the more general game from the more particular game. It will be explained in Chapter 4 how this method of analysis made it possible to compute a generalisation index for each subject and/or group of subjects.

(d) *Index of operationality*

Different subjects adopted different strategies in coping with the problem of predicting the outcome of combinations of states and operators. Some subjects tended to try the same operator several times over to see what happened. Such behaviour we called operational behaviour, because we thought that the subject was investigating how the operator was functioning. To obtain the operator index for a subject, we first identified those parts of his performance where he used the same operator three or more times in a row. We then added up all the plays included in such runs of three or more and divided this total by the total number of instances allowed, which in most games was 140. This proportion, expressed as a percentage, gave us the operationality index. The higher the percentage, the greater the operationality of the subject.

(e) *Matrix variance index*

One simple way of examining the manner in which a subject set about his task was to see whether he had explored all parts of the matrix roughly equally, or whether he had concentrated his efforts on particular parts of the matrix. Clearly, if he had spread his efforts evenly, this would be reflected in a relatively small variance as compared with another subject who might have concentrated all his plays on one or two cells of the matrix. As will be seen later on, it was possible in fact to relate size of variance with success, in terms of errors made on the A Operation phase of the experiment.

APPENDIX TO CHAPTER 3

ERROR MATRIX

	0	1	2	3	
0	0	5	2	0	7
1	1	10	2	2	15
2	2	1	4	2	9
3	3	5	2	10	20
	6	5	2	10	51

POSITION MATRIX

	0	1	2	3
0	0	119	12	0
1	31	100	11	84
2	32	120	94	28
3	62	101	68	91

FREQUENCY MATRIX

	0	1	2	3
0	9	8	4	1
1	2	15	3	8
2	2	7	10	4
3	9	13	10	15

INSTANCE MATRIX

	0	1	2	3	
0	0	8	2	0	22
1	2	14	2	7	27
2	2	7	7	2	23
3	4	13	3	14	45
	12	43	21	25	

Subject no. 37. Four game. 120 goes

4

Transfer

Some relationships between the structures embodied in the experimental tasks

There are several different kinds of relationships between the structures used in these experiments. They have already been discussed in the mathematical chapter, but will be reviewed again now. One relationship is recursion. There are two kinds of recursion: generalisation and particularisation. Generalisation is the extension of a particular structure to a wider structure which follows the same rule of generation as the first structure. For example, if the first structure is a cyclic group of order 5, that is, with five elements, then we can generalise to a cyclic group of order 7. This keeps the same generating rule, but the rule generates more elements. Another example might be the Klein group (which is the 2-by-2 group); this can be generalised into the 2-by-2-by-2 group.

The 2-by-2-by-2 structure is similar in its generation to the 2-by-2 structure, except that the former has three generators while the latter has only two.

The rules

$$x.x = \textit{neutral}$$
$$y.y = \textit{neutral}$$
$$x.y = y.x$$

generate the set of elements (*neutral*, x, y, xy).

The rules

$$x.x = y.y = z.z = \textit{neutral}$$
$$xy = yx,\ xz,\ yz = zy$$

generate the set of elements (*neutral*, x, y, z, xy, xz, yz, xyz.). The 7-element cyclic group is similar in generation to the 5-element group, but generates more elements.

The rule

$$x.x.x.x.x.x.x = \textit{neutral}$$

generates the elements

$$(\textit{neutral}, x, xx, xxx, xxxx, xxxxx, xxxxxx)$$

which are the elements of the 7-group, while the rule

$$x.x.x.x.x = \textit{neutral}$$

generates the elements

$$(\textit{neutral}, x, xx, xxx, xxxx)$$

To sum up: generalisation is the process of learning how to pass from simpler to more complex structures which have the same generating rules. And the reverse process—for example, passing from the cyclic 5 to the cyclic 3—is particularisation.

The second relationship investigated in these experiments is embeddedness. There are two kinds of embeddedness, simple and multiple. Structure A is said to be simply embedded in structure B if A has just one isomorphic image within the structure B. In other words, A is a part of B if you ignore the differences due to isomorphism. Multiple embeddedness is when there are *several* isomorphic images of A in B.

We remind the reader that a structure has an isomorphic image if what happens in it is an exact correlate of what happens in another structure. Now in every structure we have studied there is a binary operation: to any two elements in it there corresponds a third element. For example, if the pair of elements (x, y) has a corresponding element z in one structure, then, assuming that the elements which correspond to x, y and z in the isomorphic image are denoted by x^1, y^1, and z^1, in the isomorphic image structure the pair (x^1, y^1) has a corresponding element z^1. If this happens for every pair (x, y) in one structure when translated into the other structure, then we say that the two structures are *isomorphic*.

On this basis, we can see that there is a clear example of embeddedness between the 3-group and the cyclic 6-group, between the 3-group and the 9-group, and also between the 3-group and the 3-by-3 group. These will be noticed in the diagrams, as well as in the relationships obtaining in the 3-by-3 group.

In all these groups there can be found certain sets of three elements which, used in conjunction with each other, will generate only those three elements. The rule structure of the relationships between these three elements is exactly the same as the rule structure defining the group with three elements. The symbols used in the 6-group may not be the same as the symbols used in the 3-group. Nevertheless, functionally, the relationships involved are the same. In other words, there is an *isomorphism* between any representation of the 3-group and a particular representation of the 3-group detected as a subgroup of the 6-group or the 9-group or the 3-by-3 group. It is a simple *embeddedness* in the 6-group, since there is only one isomorphic picture of the 3-group in the 6-group. If there were more than one isomorphic picture it would be a *multiple embeddedness*. For example, the 2-group is multiply embedded in the Klein group because in the Klein group there are three 2-groups, each of which is a subgroup of the Klein group. Therefore, each of them is isomorphic to any representation of the 2-group.

From the point of view of learning, the embeddedness can be used in two ways: the structure used for the first task may be embedded in the structure used for the second task, or the other way around. In each of these cases we may use simple embeddedness or multiple embeddedness. So there are four ways in which embeddedness can be used: simple first embedded in second; simple second embedded in first; multiple first embedded in second; multiple second embedded in first.

The third kind of relationship is overlapping. This is related to embeddedness—in fact, embeddedness is a particular case of overlapping. The relationship of overlapping means that there is a common structure which is a part of two structures. According to this definition, embedded structures are also overlapping structures. We can distinguish between overlapping and genuine overlapping. Structures A and B are genuinely overlapping, if there is a common structure which is isomorphic to part of A as well as to a part of B, but not to the whole of A and not to the whole of B. Again, we can speak of simple overlapping and multiple overlapping. *Simple overlapping* means that there is only one structure common to both, in other words, there is only one isomorphic image of a part of one in a part of the other. *Multiple overlapping* means that there is more than one isomorphic image of one structure in the other. This may or may not operate both ways: a part of A may have several isomorphic images in B and a part of B may have several isomorphic images in A; alternatively, only one of these may be the case. In either event, we speak of *multiple overlapping.*

We give below a list of the various relationships that were used in the order in which the tasks were in fact presented to various groups of subjects.

Task I	*Task II*		*Task III*		*Task IV*
Klein 4	3	→ Recursion (generalisation) →	5	→ Recursion (generalisation) →	7
Klein 4	5	→ Recursion (particularisation) →	3	→ Recursion (generalisation) →	7
Klein 4	3	→ Recursion (generalisation) plus Embeddedness (simple) →	6	→ Recursion (generalisation) plus Overlap (simple) →	9
Klein 4	3	→ Recursion (generalisation) plus Embeddedness (simple) →	6	→ Overlap (multiple) →	9A
Klein 4	6	→ Recursion (particularisation) plus Embeddedness (simple in reverse) →	3	→ Recursion (generalisation by a factor) plus Embeddedness (simple) →	9
Klein 4	6	→ Recursion (particularisation) plus Embeddedness (simple in reverse) →	3	→ Embeddedness (multiple) →	9A

Structural relations between groups

We must now discuss in more detail the relationships between the various groups, which we have summarised diagrammatically.

(a) *Relations between the three game, five game and seven game*

In our experiments, some subjects followed the order: three game/five game/seven game, and others followed the order five game/three game/seven game. The 3-group, the 5-group and the 7-group do not include each other, nor do they overlap, except in the neutral element. (We have not counted the overlapping of neutral elements as overlapping, since we have only used groups and every group must have a neutral element.) Thus, when we pass from 3 to 5 we extend the structure. This is a recursive process and, therefore, a generalisation. When we pass from 5 to 7 again, we pass from the cyclic 5 to the more extensive cyclic 7. Again this is recursive and a generalisation. In the 5–3–7 order, we have a passage from the 5 to 3 which is recursive, but a particularisation. The 5-group and the 3-group have the same kind of generation rule, but the 3 is more particular than the 5, and less extensive. From the 3 to 7 we pass very rapidly from a small group to a very large group, i.e. instead of making the number of elements two more, we make it four more. This increases the number of triads to be learned enormously. It will be seen that this bigger leap has a considerable effect on the learning.

(b) *Relations between the three game, six game and nine game*

It will be remembered that there is another sequence used in the experimental design, running from the 3-group through the 6-group to the 9-group. Here we have a more complex situation because the 6-group, although it is cyclic (and consequently the passage from 3 to 6 is a recursion), also uses an embeddedness. The 6-group has the 3-group as a subgroup, so that passing from the 3-group to the 6-group involves simple embeddedness as well as recursion. Passing from the 6-group to the 9-group, if it is the cyclic 9-group, we again take a recursive step as we increase the size of the structure from a 6-element to a 9-element structure. There is, however, an overlap between the cyclic 6 and the cyclic 9, in the shape of the 3-group. In this case we are dealing with a recursion and a simple overlap—simple, because there is only one 3-group which is a subgroup of the 6-group and only one 3-group which is a subgroup of the cyclic 9-group.

An alternative sequence started with the 6-group, followed by the 3-group, followed by the 9-group. In this case, passing from the 6-group to the 3-group is certainly a recursive step because both these groups are cyclic and we are passing from a larger structure to a smaller one of the same kind. It is, of course, a particularisation since the 3-group is a more particular structure than the 6-group. There is also an embeddedness, but in this case the second task is embedded in the first task. So, in passing from the 6-group to the 3-group, we are dealing with embeddedness and particularisation. In passing from the 3-group to the 9-group, we again have embeddedness, a simple embeddedness since the 3-group is embedded once in the cyclic 9-group, and also recursion, since the cyclic 9-group has the same structure of cyclic change as does the 3-group. A possible complication is that the 9-group is not a mere 'increment' on the 3-group, for the number of its elements can be obtained by multiplying the number of elements of the 3-group by a factor. This may or may not have an effect on learning.

(c) *Relations between the three game, six game and nine A game*

Finally, we must deal with the 9A-group, which is the 3-by-3 group. The design included it in the sequences 3–6–9A and 6–3–9A. Passing from the 6-group to the 9A-group does not involve generalisation, because the 3-by-3 group is not cyclic. We are now passing on to a *different kind* of structure, generated by a different kind of rule. Since this gives it four subgroups which are 3-groups, we are here dealing with an *overlap* of a multiple character: there is one 3-group in the 6-group, and there are four 3-groups in the 9A-group. Thus, the second task has four isomorphic images of a part of the first task, whereas the first task has only one isomorphic picture of part of the second task.

In the sequence 6–3–9A, passing from the 3-group to the 9A-group involves a multiple embeddedness.

Methods of assessing degree of transfer between structures

It is conventional to assess degree of transfer, either by measuring the performance on all of the tasks which are given to each subject and comparing the total performances, or by comparing the performances on a given task, in relation to the particular treatments that have been given before that task. In our analysis we followed both methods, and it will be seen that the general trend is consistent, whichever way the comparisons are made. As indicated in Chapter 3, the three performance-measures upon which the comparisons are based are the A Operation score, the Equation score, and the B Operation score. The A Operation score gives the number of errors made by the subject, in the course of the learning phase of the experiment, on a predetermined number of plays. The Equation score, it was hoped, would provide some measure of the understanding which the subject had achieved of the structure of the task. The B Operation score may be regarded as a measure of the degree of learning achieved by the subject during the A Operation.

This particular measure is perhaps, under certain conditions, the least reliable of the three, because the way in which it was presented to the subjects in the machine was likely, particularly in the case of the cyclic groups, to give a clue to the way in which the structure hung together. And, indeed, there is evidence that this was the case in the performance on, for example, the cyclic 9-group and the 3-by-3 9-group.

If we are comparing performances on the same group, but given under different treatment conditions, it is legitimate to use the raw scores in each of the measures described above. However, where we wish to compare performance between groups with different numbers of elements as well as with different treatments, we must make a correction to the number of combinations correctly predicted in the B phase of the experiment. As the size of the group changes, the number of combinations that might be expected to be correctly predicted by chance will vary accordingly. In order to compute the percentage validly, we have used the method of computation set out in Chapter 3, page 55, the section headed *The Equation score*, that is where the situation is considered in which a subject is asked N questions, each with p alternative answers.

What is being transferred?

In the experimental machine, the symbol appearing in the 'State' window has been termed the Stimulus (S). The play with which the subject responds to this is termed the Response (R), and the next symbol appearing in the 'State' window has been called the Outcome (O). It is possible to interpret the learning process either in terms of a Stimulus-Response theory, according to which the subject is learning to associate an outcome O to the S and his own R, that is, to associate certain triads of S–R–O, or as the discovery of the role of certain operators within a structure. In this case, what the particular Stimuli or Responses or Outcomes are will not noticeably affect the learning because he is not so much considering what goes with what to give what, as learning what role this or that element plays when used against a variety of states of the machine.

As the subject passes from task to task, different cells in the matrices may have the same or different properties. Under an S–R interpretation we mean by 'same' that a certain response on the play dial has a specific symbol outcome in the 'State' window. Under the role interpretation, we should mean that, independently of the symbols used, if play x, acting on window y, and producing window z in one task is part of a set of relationships to which there is an exact analogue in the other task, such that if x^1, y^1, z^1 in the second task play the role of x, y, z in the first task, then the cell (x^1, y^1) in the second task 'is the same' as the cell (x, y) in the first task.

I. SOME ROLE INTERPRETATIONS OF TRANSFER

First of all we should note that in every single one of the tasks there are certain role structures which are 'the same'. Thus, in every task there is a neutral element. If the neutral acts as an operator, it induces no change, that is, it produces the same outcome as the stimulus operated on: if the neutral acts as the stimulus, any operator will produce the same outcome as that operator. This psychological interpretation corresponds to the mathematical description of the properties of the neutral element, i.e. if N is neutral and X is any other element in the group, $NX=X$ and $XN=X$. *And these properties are true of all the tasks.*

There is another way in which all the tasks are alike from the point of view of role. If the subject selects a play whose symbol lies at the same distance from the neutral as the symbol in the 'State' window, but on the opposite side, then the outcome will be the neutral. *This is true of all the tasks (except the Klein group).*

Let us term the area of each matrix covered by the above rules the *constant role area.*

In order to clarify, we must introduce a more unified notation than the subjects were given during the experiments. We will denote the neutral element by the numeral 1, and the elements on one side of the neutral by X, and on the other side by Y. If there is more than one, suffixes will show the difference. For example, in the 3-group we shall have Y on the left, I as the neutral, and X on the right. In the 5-group, we shall have Y_2, Y_1, I, X_1, X_2. In the 7-group, we shall have Y_3, Y_2, Y_1, I, X_1, X_2, X_3.

In the 3-group, if a subject has interpreted

X acting upon X=Y
and *Y acting upon Y=X*

then this interpretation does not generalise to the 5-group; but if he has decided that there is an X cycle (*I to X, X to Y, Y to I*) and a Y cycle (*I to Y, Y to X, X to I*) then he might interpret 'doing an X' as meaning taking one step around the X cycle, and 'doing a Y' as taking one step around the Y cycle. This interpretation generalises both to the 5-group and the 7-group, and, indeed, to any cyclic group. We shall term the first type of interpretation the *narrow role interpretation*, and the consideration of the cycles the *wide role interpretation*. Any subject who has interpreted the task in the wide sense is likely to generalise to a higher group much more easily than one who has taken the narrow interpretation. It also seems probable that the cyclic interpretation is more likely to occur when there is a larger number of instances from which to generalise. If the cycle has five steps, it seems *a priori* probable that it is more easily detected than if it only has three. Whether it is more easily detected when it has seven or a larger number of steps remains to be seen experimentally.

To resume, in generalising from the 3-group to the 5-group, the only role-relationships which need to be relearned in the 5-group on the narrow interpretation are X acting on $X=Y$, and Y acting on $Y=X$. (For short, we shall now say X^2 instead of 'X acting on X', and Y^2 instead of 'Y acting on Y'.)

Let us, then, look at the 5-group. This consists of the set of elements (Y_2, Y_1, I, X_1, X_2) where I denotes the neutral. It will be seen that the following relations transfer directly, on the narrow role interpretation, to the 7-group:

$$X_1^2=X_2,\ Y_1^2=Y_2,\ X_1Y_2=Y_1,\ Y_2X_1=Y_1,\ X_2Y_1=X_1,\ Y_1X_2=X_1.$$

On the other hand, it will be seen by referring to the matrices of the 5-group and the 7-group that the following relationships, on the narrow role interpretation, do *not* generalise to the 7-group. These are:

$$X_1X_2=Y_2,\ X_2X_1=Y_2,\ X_2^2=Y_1,\ Y_2^2=X_1,\ Y_1Y_2=X_2,\ Y_2Y_1=X_2.$$

On the narrow interpretation, there are six relationships that will transfer, and six that will have to be relearned. On the wide interpretation, there will be nothing to relearn because, if the interpretation is that X_1 means taking one step in the cycle (Y_2, Y_1, I, X_1, X_2), it is obvious that, every time an X_1 operator is operating on any member of the cycle, the outcome moves the S one step along this cycle. Likewise, Y_1 will move the S one step in the opposite direction along the cycle. The operator X_2 will move the S two steps in one direction, and Y_2 will move the S two steps in the other direction. All these operations transfer bodily into the 7-group, since all that the subject has to add is that there is also an X_3 and a Y_3.

Whether any subject did in fact think in terms of one or the other of these interpretations, or whether he thought in terms of triads, i.e. simply as S-R-O material, it is not possible to tell directly. We shall, however, describe the situation in terms of all three hypotheses and see which fits the observed facts the closest.

Let us examine what happens when the 5-group is followed by the 3-group. As already stated, the wide role interpretation is more likely to have been achieved if the cycle is longer. Also the chance of learning that an $X_nY_n=I$ (that is, neutral) is twice as good in the 5-group as it is in the 3-group. Consequently, it is twice as probable that this relationship will be transferred from the 5-group to the 3-group, than from the 3-group to the 5-group. It seems likely, therefore, that learning the 5-group will result in considerable economy in the eventual learning of the 3-group. We find that this is indeed so in the case of the children, but there is no such effect observable with the adults. Why this should be so, we shall attempt to explain later.

After the 5-group matrix, the only new rules in the 3-group matrix on the narrow role interpretation are $X_1X_1=Y_1$ and $Y_1Y_1=X_1$. So the subject only has to learn two relationships in order to interpret the 3-group task; he knows the rest already.

There are some special considerations applicable to the passage from the 3-group to the 7-group. Anybody who makes this passage will, in our design, already have learned, or at least had contact with, the 5-group. The combinations $X_1X_1=X_2$ and $Y_1Y_1=Y_2$ are met with in the 5-group; they need to be unlearned in the 3-group, and relearned for the 7-group. It is conceivable that this part of the matrix will cause more difficulties than the rest. Apart from this, however, the rest of the 3-group matrix is in the constant role area. Passing from the 3-group to the 7-group is thus in a sense almost the same psychological process as passing from the 5-group to the 7-group, except that two combinations will have to be learned and unlearned and relearned.

Let us now consider the learning which takes place when we pass from the 3-group to the 6-group. Apart from the constant role area, which consists here of sixteen combinations, there are the combinations $X_1^2=X_2$ and $Y_1^2=Y_2$ to be relearned. This leaves another eighteen combinations to learn. An additional form of relationship between the structures here is embeddedness, since the group (Y_2, I, X_2) is embedded in the group $(Y_3, Y_2, Y_1, I, X_1, X_2)$, that is, the first is a subgroup of the second. Out of this could come the realisation that $Y_2^2=X_2$ and $X_2^2=Y_2$ are a form of transfer from the 3-group relationships, which were true for the 3-group (Y, I, X), but are not true now of $Y_1^2=X_1$

and $X_1^2=Y_1$. This realisation is all the more likely since the symbols used were adapted to it, the same shapes being used in the subgroup of the 6-group as were used in the original 3-group for the first original learning, even though all the symbols used in the 3-group subgroup of the 6-group were yellow, whereas two of them were red shapes in the original 3-group.

If, then, the subject realises the embeddedness, he has sixteen more combinations to learn; if not, he has eighteen more to learn. Of course, on the wide role interpretation, if the cycle $(Y_1, I, X_1, Y_1, I, X_1)$ has been learned, this can be extended to the larger cycle $(Y_3, Y_2, Y_1, I, X_1, X_2, X_3, Y_3, Y_2, I, X_1, X_2$, etc.). On the other hand, if it has not been learned, then either the narrow role interpretation has been learned, or possibly only the S–R combinations are being associated with the appropriate outcomes.

In the case of passage from the 6-group to the 3-group, there is a possibility of transfer of the subgroup (Y_2, I, X_2) to the 3-group (Y_1, I, X_1). If this transfer does occur, there is no reason for any errors to be made at all in the 3-group. If this 'bodily' transfer does not occur, it is necessary to relearn that X_1^2 is now Y_1 and that Y_1^2 is now X_1.

We must now describe the passage from the 6-group to the cyclic 9-group. Here, the common role area consists of twenty-five combinations. If the subgroup (Y_2, I, X_2) has been transferred to the subgroup (Y_3, I, X_3), there are four combinations that do not need to be learned. If the 6-group is followed by the 3-group and then by the 9-group, there are two combinations which have to be unlearned, namely $X_1^2=X_2$, $Y_1^2=Y_2$, which hold in the 6-group, whereas in the 3-group $X_1^2=Y_1$ and $Y_1^2=X_1$. Then, when the 9-group follows the 6-group, they have to relearn that $X_1^2=X_2$ and $Y_1^2=Y_2$. In other words, the common role area contains twenty-five combinations, the subgroup (if it has been learned) contains four, and two have to be relearned, which makes thirty-one. In all, there are fifty more combinations to learn.

In the main diagonal of the 6 to 9A sequence, that is, in cases where the stimuli are represented by the same symbol as the responses, these responses, together with the common role area, exactly cover the area taken up by the four subgroups. There is no relearning at all in this case. The common role area consists of twenty-seven combinations; if the subgroup (Y_3, I, X_3) has already been learned, that adds two more, making twenty-nine in all. If all the subgroups have been transferred from the previous three groups, it means that thirty-three combinations are already known, and forty-eight are still to be learnt to complete the task.

2. THE GROUP MATRICES LABELLED ACCORDING TO THE ROLE INTERPRETATIONS

In the matrix diagrams that follow, the following abbreviations are used to indicate the way in which each cell of the matrix is related to the previously encountered games:

C=Common Core R=Relearning
E=Extrapolation N=New
G=Generalisation

Narrow role interpretations

3-group following 4-group

	Y_1	I	X_1
Y	R	C	R
I	C	C	C
X_1	R	C	R

It is likely that the 4-group is thought of, by most subjects who think in any way about roles, as split into

(a) the neutral (b) the others.

The way in which the neutral and the others combine, or the neutral combines with the neutral, is a part of the common role area. This is valid for the 3-group also.

In the 4-group the 'others' are related to the remaining 'others' in the following way:

(a) In the case of the 'squares', the outcome is always the neutral.

(b) In the case of the 'non-squares', the outcome is always a non-neutral.

In the case of the 3-group this latter breakup is exactly in the opposite sense. This means that for the 3-group:

(a) For the 'squares' the outcome is always a non-neutral.

(b) For the 'non-squares', the outcome is always a neutral.

The 'carry over' or 'same' part of the 3-matrix is therefore only that part of it which relates the neutral and non-neutral as stimuli and responses to the outcomes.

5-group following 4-group

	Y_2	Y_1	I	X_1	X_2
Y_2	N	N	C	N	N
Y_1	N	N	C	N	N
I	C	C	C	C	C
X_1	N	N	C	N	N
X_2	N	N	C	N	N

5-group following 3-group

	Y_2	Y_1	I	X_1	X_2
Y_2	G	G	E	G	E
Y_1	G	R	C	C	G
I	E	C	C	C	E
X_1	G	C	C	R	G
X_2	E	G	E	G	G

7-group following 5-group, taking into account only the *immediately* preceding task.

	Y_3	Y_2	Y_1	I	X_1	X_2	X_3
Y_3	G	G	G	E	G	G	E
Y_2	G	R	R	C	C	C	G
Y_1	G	R	C	C	C	C	G
I	E	C	C	C	C	C	E
X_1	G	C	C	C	C	R	G
X_2	G	C	C	C	R	R	G
X_3	E	G	G	E	G	G	G

7-group following 3-group, taking into account only the *immediately* preceding task.

	Y_3	Y_2	Y_1	I	X_1	X_2	X_3
Y_3	G	G	G	E	G	G	E
Y_2	G	G	G	E	G	E	G
Y_1	G	G	R	C	C	G	G
I	E	E	C	C	C	E	E
X_1	G	G	C	C	R	G	G
X_2	G	E	G	E	G	G	G
X_3	E	G	G	E	G	G	G

9-group preceded by 6-group and 3-group, or by 3-group and 6-group, taking into account both preceding tasks.

	Y_4	Y_3	Y_2	Y_1	I	X_1	X_2	X_3	X_4
Y_4	G	G	G	G	E	G	G	G	E
Y_3	G	R	R	R	C	C	C	E	G
Y_2	G	R	R	C	C	C	C	G	G
Y_1	G	R	C	C	C	C	C	G	G
I	E	C	C	C	C	C	C	E	E
X_1	G	C	C	C	C	C	R	G	G
X_2	G	C	C	C	C	R	R	G	G
X_3	G	E	G	G	E	G	G	G	G
X_4	E	G	G	G	E	G	G	G	G

Interpretation of the 9A-group

The narrow role interpretation still functions to some extent, based on the supposition (explicit or implicit) that the group is cyclic. The 'common role area' in this task is still the same as in all the other tasks (with the exception of the Klein group).

9A-group (3-by-3 *Nine*), preceded by 3-group and 6-group in that order.

	Y_4	Y_3	Y_2	Y_1	I	X_1	X_2	X_3	X_4
Y_4	C	N	N	N	C	N	N	N	C
Y_3	N	C	R	R	C	C	R	C	N
Y_2	N	R	C	C	C	R	C	N	N
Y_1	N	R	C	C	C	C	R	N	N
I	C	C	C	C	C	C	C	C	C
X_1	N	C	R	C	C	C	R	N	N
X_2	N	R	R	R	C	R	C	N	N
X_3	N	C	N	N	C	N	N	C	N
X_4	C	N	N	N	C	N	N	N	C

9A-group (3-by-3 *Nine*), preceded by 6-group and 3-group in that order.

	Y_4	Y_3	Y_2	Y_1	I	X_1	X_2	X_3	X_4
Y_4	C	N	N	N	C	N	N	N	C
Y_3	N	C	R	R	C	C	R	C	N
Y_2	N	R	C	C	C	R	C	N	N
Y_1	N	R	C	R	C	C	R	N	N
I	C	C	C	C	C	C	C	C	C
X_1	N	C	R	C	C	R	R	N	N
X_2	N	R	R	R	C	R	C	N	N
X_3	N	C	N	N	C	N	N	C	N
X_4	C	N	N	N	C	N	N	N	C

Since the 9A is a non-cyclic group, there is a much more appropriate interpretation in terms of the *two generators* of the group. Variation of colour was used to indicate the successive application of one of the generators, and variation of shape the successive application of the other. If the subject has learned not to make any errors in the colour scheme, he has presumably realised how one of the generators functions within the group. If he has learned not to make any errors in the shape scheme, he has presumably realised the role of the other generator. The colour scheme is as follows:

	orange	yellow	red
orange	red	orange	yellow
yellow	orange	yellow	red
red	yellow	red	orange

The shape scheme is as follows:

	triangle	circle	square
triangle	square	triangle	circle
circle	triangle	circle	square
square	circle	square	triangle

When the subject has learned both the shape and the colour scheme, he will have formulated the *wide role interpretation* most appropriate to this structure. Measures of the tendency to learn the functioning of one or the other of the generators will be given later.

Role interpretations of the 6-group

6-group, narrow role, when preceded by 4-group and conceived as a 6-by-1 group.

	Y_3	Y_2	Y_1	I	X_1	X_2
Y_3	C	N	N	C	N	N
Y_2	N	N	N	C	N	N
Y_1	N	N	N	C	N	N
I	C	C	C	C	C	C
X_1	N	N	N	C	N	N
X_2	N	N	N	C	N	N

6-group, narrow role, when preceded by 4-group and conceived as a 2-by-3 group.

	Y_3	Y_2	Y_1	I	X_1	X_2
Y_3	C	G	G	C	G	G
Y_2	G	G	C	C	G	G
Y_1	G	C	G	C	G	G
I	C	C	C	C	C	C
X_1	G	G	G	C	G	G
X_2	G	G	G	C	G	G

G=Generalisation from 2-by-2 to 2-by-3.

Narrow role interpretation of the 6-group when preceded by the 3-group.

	Y_3	Y_2	Y_1	I	X_1	X_2
Y_3	G	G	G	E	G	G
Y_2	G	G	G	E	G	E
Y_1	G	G	R	C	C	G
I	E	E	C	C	C	E
X_1	G	G	C	C	R	G
X_2	G	E	G	E	G	G

Some comments on the foregoing narrow role interpretations

(a) *Narrow role interpretations of the 6-group.* There are two possible interpretations, the (6) interpretation when the group is conceived as a cycle Y_3, Y_2, Y_1, I, X_1, X_2 . . ., and the (6a) interpretation when the group is conceived as a direct product of I, x, xx and y, yx, yxx.

By the narrow role interpretation of the 6-group we mean the sum total of relationships that can be immediately deduced from the realisation of the relative positions of the elements—relative, that is, to the neutral element.

For example:

$$X_1 . X_1 = X_2 \text{ and } Y_1 . Y_1 = Y_2$$

can be expressed by the narrow role interpretation as:

'One away from the neutral played against itself gives you two away from the neutral on the same side.'

The wide role interpretation would be:

'Playing the first one next to the neutral will give you the next state to the one played against in the direction in which the play is from the neutral; the cycle $(Y_3, Y_2, Y_1, I, X_1, X_2, Y_3, Y_2, \ldots)$ must of course be considered as closed.'

It will be seen that the 'wide role' interpretation is more general, in that it makes possible six correct predictions, whereas the narrow role makes possible only two correct predictions.

(b) *Narrow role interpretations of other cyclic groups.*

The 5-group (Y_2, Y_1, I, X_1, X_2),
the 7-group $(Y_3, Y_2, Y_1, I, X_1, X_2, X_3)$
and the 9-group $(Y_4, Y_3, Y_2, Y_1, I, X_1, X_2, X_3, X_4)$

are all cyclic, and the narrow role interpretation is to be treated in the same way as for the 6-group, when this is considered as a cyclic group.

As the groups get larger, it seems increasingly likely that interpretations such as:

'The first and second on the same side will give you the third one on the same side.'

or

'The first and the third on the same side will give you the fourth on the same side' (when valid, i.e. in 9-group).

and so on, will become generalised into:

'The position of the outcome is the sum of the position of the stimulus and of the response.'

Even so, this interpretation only applies *sometimes*, and so is still a narrow role interpretation, although wider than the sum total of the separate interpretations. Such a general statement will only account for all the possible outcomes if the cycle is closed, and if the subject learns to 'jump' from one end of the dial to the other, when the 'sum' becomes too large to stay on the dial. This is, in fact, the realisation of the cyclic nature of the group which we have called the *wide role interpretation.* It alone accounts for all that occurs within the group.

Let us take the case of a subject considering a 5-task as a cycle. Such a consideration is more likely to occur with the 5-group than with the 3-group as there are many more instances in the 5-group than in the 3-group. Its cyclic nature is, therefore, *a priori* more likely to appear to him than in the 3-group.

From the narrow role structural point of view we have thought of the 5-group as being determined by certain relationships between parts of the matrix. It will be recalled that the relationships that are valid for all the groups used in the series of experiments are (1) the properties of the neutral, and (2) the property $X_nY_n=I$. By looking at the matrices for the 5-group and the 3-group it can easily be verified that the $X_nY_n=I$ relationship is obtainable twice as often in the 5-group as it is in the 3-group, even on the hypothesis of random choice. In the 3-group there is only $XY=I$, in the 5-group there is $X_1Y_1=I$ and $X_2Y_2=I$. Equally, for the neutral, as well as $X_1 . I=X_1$ we have $X_2I=X_2$; and so also for the Y stimuli.

The chance of these particular formulations arising is thus greater in the 5-group than in the 3-group. It seems, therefore, that in the 5–3 treatment it is likely that the 'cyclic' insight occurs sooner than in the 3–5 treatment so that it is predictable that less errors will be made. If we look ahead to the results, we see that this is nevertheless not the case with the adults, though it is with the children. One might deduce that the adults are able to use the minimal information from the 3-group and apply it more skilfully in the 5-group than the children can. In the 5–3 treatment, the children appear to be given enough experience in the 5-group to gain these insights so that their performance matches the performance of the adults.

Generalisation and role interpretations

It is clear from this study, and from the previous study also, that children find it much more difficult to generalise than adults, but are able to particularise. This again leads one to expect that children will do relatively better on the 5–3 than on the 3–5 treatment.

On the *wide role interpretation*, the cyclic interpretation is less likely in the 5-task than in the 3-task. But it is unlikely, *a priori*, that a sufficient number of subjects consider the 5-task cyclic to account for the observed difference in the results. In any case, there seems to be no difference between the adults under the two different treatments, the 3–5 and the 5–3.

The reason that the adults do better on the 3–5 order than the children, in comparison to how they each do on the 5–3 order, is probably that the adults are more able to cope with the actual pieces of generalisation that they have to perform in order to organise a 'cognitive map' of the 5-matrix, given a 'cognitive map' of the 3-matrix. The adults' performance on the generalisation section of the 5-matrix, on the narrow role interpretation, should correlate better with 'understanding' than with performance on the whole matrix. As the children are more likely to be playing the generalisation part of the matrix as a task of learning to associate triads, one would not expect this differential with the children; in fact, in their case, one would expect the performance on the whole matrix to be a better predictor of 'understanding' than any one part of it.

To measure the extent of 'understanding', it is convenient to use the scores obtained on the equations. By 'understanding' is meant that the relationships 'understood' can be put to use, i.e. that they have become *operational* or *reversible* in Piaget's sense. To solve an equation, the subject needs to reverse the situation of learning the outcome to a certain pair of antecedents, and we may take ability to do this as a measure of the subjects' 'understanding'. As to performance level, this is clearly tested on the B Operation.

The following table indicates how Equation scores (E), B Operation scores (B) and Generalisation scores (G) intercorrelate. The Generalisation scores (G) are based on the subjects' performances on those cells of the matrices which were labelled G in the tables given earlier in this chapter.

	Adults *(4–3)5*	*Children* *(4–3)5*	*Adults* *(4)5*	*Children* *(4)5*
E:B	0·60	0·85	0·45	0·01
E:G	0·88	0·70	0·47	0·01

TABLE 4.1 Product-moment Correlation Coefficients of 'understanding' (E), 'generalisation' (G) and 'performance' (B) measures in adults and children, compared on the 3 group and 5 group depending on order of presentation.

It is clear that the differences are in the predicted direction in the case of the 3–5 order, and that there is no difference in the 5–3 order.

3. SOME S–R THEORY INTERPRETATIONS OF TRANSFER

Any one task can be regarded as consisting of the learning of a number of triads, which consist of stimulus, response and outcome. When we analyse each task in this way, it is possible to compute the amount of learning and relearning that needs to be done from one task to the next. Tables 4.2 and 4.3 summarise the results of an analysis in these terms. Although there is some variation from task to task in what has to be relearned, the extent of this is very small compared with the total amount of new learning which is required. For example, when the nine game follows the three game (in which case the six game will also have been experienced), four of the triad combinations are the same as in the previous games, twelve are different, and the remaining sixty-five are new (Table 4.2). If we take only those triads as relevant which were encountered in the previous game, then one triad is the same, two are different and seventy-nine are new. When the nine-A game follows the six game and the three game, fifteen triads are the same, twenty-one are different and the remaining forty-five are new; on the other hand, if we consider only the immediately preceding game as relevant, then one triad is the same, three are different and seventy-seven are new. We maintain that, on the hypothesis that only what was encountered in the immediately preceding game is relevant, the amount of new material so completely swamps the amount which is either the same or different, that the small amount which is not new will affect the overall results of the transfer experiments very little.

Finally, it is extremely unlikely that a subject will remember any substantial number of triads *learned as triads* two or three days previously. From the S-R point of view, the consideration of the immediately preceding task is the most appropriate formulation of the problem.

4. THE GROUP MATRICES LABELLED ACCORDING TO TRIAD LEARNING INTERPRETATIONS

There now follows a 'stimulus analysis' of the matrices of the groups, in which we fully take into account the nature of the stimulus material which was presented to the subjects and upon which the triad learning was assumed to take place. We shall distinguish the following categories of triad:

(S) The stimuli, correct responses and outcomes are represented by the same symbols in the new task as in the old task from which the transfer effects are being studied.

(R_1) In the new task, the stimulus is different from the stimulus in the old task; the correct response is the same as in the old task; the outcome is the same as in the old task.

(R_2) The stimulus in the new task is the same as in the old task; the correct response is different from the correct response in the old task; the outcome is the same as in the old task.

(R_3) The stimulus in the new task is the same as in the old task; the correct response is the same as in the old task; but the outcome in the new task is different from the outcome in the old task.

(N) At least two of the three components, i.e. stimulus, correct response, outcome, are different in the new task from what they were in the old task.

It might be considered that only the R_3 type of triad represents 'real' relearning, as in this a different association must be formed to an already established association of outcome to stimulus-response pair. It could be argued that an R_3 triad is therefore more difficult to learn than either an R_1 or an R_2 or an N triad. It should now be possible to grade the difficulty of the tasks in terms of the numbers of the different kinds of triads encountered by subjects during the learning being considered. We can make the assumptions: either

(a) that only the immediately preceding task needs to be taken into account to determine these categories; or

(b) that all the previously performed tasks need to be taken into account in determining the triad categories.

We might call these different ways of assessing the difficulty of a series of tasks:

(a) the narrow S–R assessment of task difficulty
(b) the extended S–R assessment of task difficulty.

One might argue that any very small differences which exist between the tasks (when assessed in this way) because of what has to be learned and relearned are negligible. However, for the sake of completeness, we include below both types of tables to enable the reader to compare for himself the two methods of analysis (Tables 4.2 and 4.3).

Matrix diagrams giving the appropriate numbers of the different kinds of triads in all the series, on either supposition, are also given below:

Learning and relearning on an S–R basis

3-group preceded by 4-group—(4)3

	Y_1	I	X_1
Y_1	R_3	S	R_2
I	S	S	N
X_1	R_1	N	N

3-group preceded by 5-group or 6-group—(5)3 and (6)3

	Y_1	I	X_1
Y_1	R_3	S	S
I	S	S	S
X_1	S	S	R_3

5-group preceded by 4-group—(4)5

	Y_2	Y_1	I	X_1	X_2
Y_2	N	N	N	R_1	N
Y_1	N	R_3	R_2	R_3	R_2
I	N	R_1	N	R_1	N
X_1	R_2	R_3	R_2	R_3	N
X_2	N	R_1	N	N	N

5-group preceded by 4-group and 3-group—(4–3)5

	Y_2	Y_1	I	X_1	X_2
Y_2	N	R_1	N	R_1	N
Y_1	R_2	R_3	R_2	R_3	N
I	N	R_1	N	R_1	R_1
X_1	R_2	R_3	R_2	S	R_3
X_2	N	N	R_2	R_3	R_3

7-group preceded by 3-group and 5-group—(3–5)7

	Y_3	Y_2	Y_1	I	X_1	X_2	X_3
Y_3	N	R_1	N	N	R_1	R_1	N
Y_2	R_2	R_3	R_3	S	S	S	R_2
Y_1	N	R_3	S	S	S	S	R_2
I	N	S	S	S	S	S	N
X_1	R_2	S	S	S	S	R_3	N
X_2	R_2	S	S	S	R_3	R_3	R_2
X_3	N	R_1	R_1	N	N	R_1	N

7-group preceded by 5-group and 3-group—(5–3)7

	Y_3	Y_2	Y_1	I	X_1	X_2	X_3
Y_3	N	R_1	N	N	R_1	R_1	N
Y_2	R_2	R_3	R_3	S	S	S	R_2
Y_1	N	R_3	S	S	S	S	R_2
I	N	S	S	N	R_1	R_1	N
X_1	R_2	S	S	R_2	S	R_3	N
X_2	R_2	S	S	R_2	R_3	R_3	R_2
X_3	N	R_1	R_1	N	N	R_1	N

6-group preceded by 4-group and 3-group—(3)6

	Y_3	Y_2	Y_1	I	X_1	X_2
Y_3	S	R_3	R_3	S	R_2	R_2
Y_2	R_3	R_3	S	S	R_2	R_2
Y_1	R_3	S	R_3	S	S	R_2
I	S	S	S	S	S	N
X_1	R_1	R_1	S	S	R_3	R_3
X_2	R_1	R_1	R_1	N	R_1	N

6-group preceded by 4-group—(4)6

	Y_3	Y_2	Y_1	I	X_1	X_2
Y_3	S	R_3	R_3	S	R_2	R_2
Y_2	R_3	R_3	S	S	R_2	R_2
Y_1	R_3	S	R_3	S	R_2	N
I	S	S	S	S	N	N
X_1	R_1	R_1	R_1	N	N	N
X_2	R_1	R_1	N	N	N	N

9-group preceded by 6-group and 3-group in that order (but taking into account only the immediately preceding task, the 3-group)—(6)(3)9

	Y_4	Y_3	Y_2	Y_1	I	X_1	X_2	X_3	X_4
Y_4	N	N	N	N	N	N	N	N	N
Y_3	N	N	N	N	N	N	N	N	N
Y_2	N	N	N	N	N	N	N	N	N
Y_1	N	N	N	N	N	N	R_1	N	N
I	N	N	N	N	N	R_1	R_1	R_1	R_1
X_1	N	N	N	N	R_2	S	R_3	N	N
X_2	N	N	N	R_2	R_2	R_3	R_3	N	N
X_3	N	N	N	N	R_2	N	N	N	N
X_4	N	N	N	N	R_2	N	N	N	N

9A-group (3-by-3) preceded by 6-group and 3-group in that order (but taking into account only the immediately preceding task, the 3-group)—(6)(3)9A

	Y_4	Y_3	Y_2	Y_1	I	X_1	X_2	X_3	X_4
Y_4	N	N	N	N	N	N	N	N	N
Y_3	N	N	N	N	N	N	N	N	N
Y_2	N	N	N	N	N	N	N	N	N
Y_1	N	N	N	N	N	N	R_1	N	N
I	N	N	N	N	N	N	S	N	S
X_1	N	N	N	N	N	N	R_1	N	R_1
X_2	N	N	N	R_2	S	R_2	R_3	N	N
X_3	N	N	N	N	N	N	N	N	N
X_4	N	N	N	N	S	R_2	N	N	R_3

9-group preceded by 3-group and 6-group in that order (taking into account all preceding tasks)—(4–3–6)9

	Y_4	Y_3	Y_2	Y_1	I	X_1	X_2	X_3	X_4
Y_4	N	N	N	N	N	N	R_1	N	N
Y_3	N	N	N	N	N	R_1	R_1	N	N
Y_2	N	N	R_3	R_3	R_2	R_3	R_3	R_2	R_2
Y_1	N	N	R_3	S	R_2	R_3	S	R_2	N
I	N	N	R_1	R_1	N	R_1	R_1	N	N
X_1	N	R_2	R_3	R_3	R_2	R_3	R_3	N	N
X_2	R_2	R_2	R_3	S	R_2	R_3	R_3	N	N
X_3	N	N	R_1	R_1	N	N	N	N	N
X_4	N	N	R_1	N	N	N	N	N	N

9A-group (3-by-3) preceded by 3-group and 6-group in that order (taking into account all preceding tasks)—(4–3–6)9A

	Y_4	Y_3	Y_2	Y_1	I	X_1	X_2	X_3	X_4
Y_4	N	N	N	N	N	N	R_1	R_1	R_1
Y_3	N	N	N	N	N	N	R_1	R_1	R_1
Y_2	N	N	N	N	N	N	R_1	R_1	R_1
Y_1	N	N	N	S	S	S	R_3	R_3	R_3
I	N	N	N	S	S	S	S	S	S
X_1	N	N	N	S	S	S	R_3	R_3	R_3
X_2	R_2	R_2	R_2	R_3	S	R_3	R_3	R_3	R_3
X_3	R_2	R_2	R_2	R_3	S	R_3	R_3	R_3	R_3
X_4	R_2	R_2	R_2	R_3	S	R_3	R_3	R_3	R_3

5. TASK DIFFICULTY ASSESSED IN S–R TERMS

Narrow S–R assessment of task difficulty

Task difficulty assessed in terms of the numbers of triads in each task that are to be learned or relearned:

Task being assessed	*Preceding tasks*	*To be relearned*	*Same as in previous task*	*New*	*New plus relearning*
5-group	4- & 3-groups	3	1	21	24
6-group	4- & 3-groups	2	7	27	29
7-group	4-, 5- & 3-groups	3	20	26	29
9-group	4-, 6- & 3-groups	12	4	65	77
9A-group	4-, 6- & 3-groups	21	15	45	66
7-group	4-, 3- & 5-groups	6	19	24	30
9-group	4-, 3- & 6-groups	13	3	65	78
9A-group	4-, 3- & 6-groups	21	15	45	66

TABLE 4.2

Extended S–R interpretation or,
Overall triad learning interpretation analysis by tasks

Task being assessed	*Preceding tasks*	S	R_1	R_2	R_3	N	S	R_3	$R_1 + R_2 + N$	S	$R_1 + R_2 + R_3 + N$
4-group		—	—	—	—	16	—	—	16	—	16
3-group	4-group	3	1	1	1	3	3	1	5	3	6
3-group	4- & 5-groups	4	1	1	3	—	4	3	2	4	5
3-group	4- & 6-groups	7	—	—	2	—	7	2	—	7	2
5-group	4-group	—	4	4	4	13	—	4	21	—	25
5-group	4- & 3-groups	1	5	5	6	8	1	6	18	1	24
6-group	4-group	10	5	5	6	10	10	6	20	10	26
6-group	4- & 3-groups	14	6	6	7	3	14	7	15	14	22
7-group	4-, 3- & 5-groups	19	6	6	6	12	19	6	24	19	30
7-group	4-, 5- & 3-groups	14	8	8	6	13	14	6	29	14	35
9-group	4-, 3- & 6-groups	3	10	10	13	45	3	13	65	3	78
9-group	4-, 6- & 3-groups	4	10	10	12	45	4	12	65	4	77
9A-group	4-, 3- & 6-groups	15	9	9	21	27	15	21	45	15	66
9A-group	4-, 6- & 3-groups	15	9	9	21	27	15	21	45	15	66

TABLE 4.3

In the sections which follow we shall use the foregoing analyses of the amount of learning involved in each task in order to evaluate the performances of the different groups of subjects who were given tasks under the varied treatments outlined in Chapter 3.

The effects of treatment on performance

1. COMPARISON OF PERFORMANCES ON THE 3-GROUP AND 5-GROUP, DEPENDING ON ORDER OF PRESENTATION

All subjects started with the Klein group; in some cases, this was followed by the 3-group, 5-group and 7-group, and in others by the 5-group, 3-group and 7-group. Since performance on the Klein group, which was given to acquaint the subjects with the way in which the task was to be done, is found to match the groups of subjects almost exactly, it is felt unnecessary, with a few exceptions, to consider the effect of performance on this 4-element group on the tasks that followed.

We shall consider the A Operation, B Operation and Equation scores for both adults and children. We shall also consider one kind of transfer score which consists of the total number of erroneous predictions. In the present case, this will consist of the sum of all the erroneous predictions made on the 3-group and the 5-group.

The results are as follows. (It should be remembered that, on the A and B Operation scores, the higher the score, the poorer the performance. The converse is true with the Equation scores.)

A OPERATION SCORES FOR ADULTS	S.D.	A OPERATION SCORES FOR CHILDREN	S.D.
Total (3) + (5) = 64	30·5	Total (3) + (5) = 88	37·1
(5) + (3) = 59	20·3	(5) + (3) = 60	20·5
B OPERATION SCORES FOR ADULTS	**S.D.**	**B OPERATION SCORES FOR CHILDREN**	**S.D.**
Total (3) + (5) = 4·7	5·1	Total (3) + (5) = 10	5·3
(5) + (3) = 5·4	4·8	(5) + (3) = 5	4·2

EQUATION SCORES

(Number totally correct, corrected to allow for chance successes)

ADULTS	CHILDREN
Total (3) + (5) = 13	Total (3) + (5) = 9
(5) + (3) = 14	(5) + (3) = 13

TABLE 4.4

The first thing that is immediately noticed is that on all the scores for adults there is no appreciable difference between the (3)5 treatment and the (5)3 treatment. It is equally obvious that on the children's scores there is a consistent trend towards success with (5)3 treatment, both in terms of the smaller number of errors made and of the larger number of equations correctly solved. We will discuss possible reasons for this in a moment. Another clear indication in the tables is that the adults obtain consistently better scores on the (3)5 treatment than the children, but score equally with the children on the (5)3 treatment on all measures available.

It appears (as has already been noticed in *Thinking in Structures*) that children find it more difficult to generalise than adults, and that children also find it more difficult to generalise than to particularise. This is borne out by the higher scores in terms of errors for the children with the (3)5 treatment. They appear to find it difficult to pass from a smaller to a larger structure of the same kind.

On the null hypothesis we may expect an even chance of the following four possibilities occurring:

(a) the (3)5 treatment for adults is more successful than the (3)5 treatment for children, and the (5)3 treatment for adults is more successful than the (5)3 treatment for children.

(b) the (3)5 treatment for adults is *not* more successful than the (3)5 treatment for children, but the (5)3 treatment for adults is more successful than the (5)3 treatment for children.

(c) the (3)5 treatment for adults is more successful than the (3)5 treatment for children, but the (5)3 treatment for adults is *not* more successful than the (5)3 treatment for children.

(d) the (3)5 treatment for adults is *not* more successful than the (3)5 treatment for children, and the (5)3 treatment for adults is likewise *not* more successful than the (5)3 treatment for children.

Since any one of these cases is as likely to occur as the others, on the hypothesis of random play, there is one chance in four of one of these cases in fact occurring on the null hypothesis. Now we have three measures, the A Operation, the B Operation and the Equation measure, and along all these measures we have case (c) occurring. The chance of this occurring on three separate measures on the hypothesis that random answers were being given by all the subjects would be 1 in 64.

Let us look more closely into the process of passing from the 3-task to the 5-task, limiting ourselves entirely to the consideration of the stimulus material. Let us consider the (3)5 situation first. If the subject is simply learning the combinations and the corresponding outcomes, he has to learn nine triads. There are nine sets of S–R–O combinations. When the subject passes on to the 5-group, one of these S–R–O triads is the same as he had before; three of them are different, and these he will have to relearn; there are also twenty-one triads that are new. So the total number of triads he has to learn is thirty, and three triads have to be relearned. (See Table 4.2).

Now let us consider the events in the (5)3 order. The subject has first to learn twenty-five triads. When he passes on to the 3-group, then there will be one triad which is the same as he had before; three will be different, which he will have to relearn; and five others will be new. So the total number of triads he has to learn on this sequence is thirty, and again three have to be relearned. That is, on both treatments there will have to be thirty triads learned and three relearned on the restricted S–R hypothesis. It appears that, on this hypothesis, there is no reason why the (3)5 subjects should be either better or worse than the (5)3 subjects if their performance is measured by the number of errors committed.

We may next grade some series of tasks against other series on the criteria suggested, and observe whether the scores in fact obtained by the subjects do or do not substantiate the suppositions on which the grading of the difficulty was based. Table 4.5 below makes assessments of the difficulty of learning the 3-group when it is given under different conditions. The assessments of difficulty are based on the hypothesis that S-R learning only takes place. The performance measures obtained are also given alongside.

Task	*Previous experience*	*S*	$R_1+R_2+R_3+N$	*A Op.*	*S.D.*	*B Op.*	*S.D.*	*Equations*
				ADULTS				
3-group	4-group	3	6	20	11·3	1·3	2·0	6·0
3-group	4- & 5-groups	4	5	10	6·3	·1		8·3
3-group	4- & 6-groups	7	2	21	12·0	1·6	1·9	5·5
				CHILDREN				
3-group	4-group	3	6	29	14·4	2·4	2·7	5·0
3-group	4- & 5-groups	4	5	12	8·9	·8	1·87	7·0
3-group	4- & 6-groups	7	2	21	11·7	2·2	2·4	6·4

TABLE 4.5

If the performances in the course of learning the 3-group are primarily a function of the sheer amount of learning and relearning to be done, then we should expect the performances to be in the following order, going from anticipated best to poorest performance:

(a) 3 preceded by (4)6
(b) 3 preceded by 4
(c) 3 preceded by (4)5

This ordering takes account of *relearning* as well as of the number of triads that are the same as in the preceding tasks. In fact, there is a consistent indication that, whilst the 3 preceded by (4)6 performances are much like those of the 3 preceded only by the 4, nevertheless the performances on the 3 preceded by the (4)5 are much better.

2. PERFORMANCES ON THE 5-GROUP AND 6-GROUP COMPARED

It is a little difficult to compare the 5-task with the 6-task, since the 6-task contains more information to be learned than the 5-task. It can be seen, however, from the table below (Table 4.6) that, on an S–R learning hypothesis, the amount of relearning combined with the amount of new learning is not substantially different in the two cases. However, even if on this basis we might feel justified in making a direct comparison, it must be remembered that there is a large *S* area in the matrix of the 6-task. On the null hypothesis, these triads will have the same chance of being 'played' as the others. This means that, although the amount of new learning and relearning is the same, or approximately so, in the 5-task and the 6-task, subjects learning the 6-task have effectively less chance of learning this piece of new material because they are going to meet it less often during the learning period. For this reason, we might expect the 6-task to be just a little harder than the 5-task, which is borne out by the A scores. The differences in the *B* and *E* scores are probably rather too large to be explained on this basis alone.

If we look at the performance of the children, it will be seen that the prediction made fits the data somewhat better.

Task	*Previous experience*	*S*	$R_1+R_2+R_3+N$	*A Op.*	*S.D.*	*B Op.*	*S.D.*	*Equations**
			ADULTS					
5-group	4-group	—	25	48	19·1	5·3/25	4·6	5·7/10
5-group	4- & 3-groups	1	24	52	24·0	4·0/25	3·8	6·8/10
6-group	4-group	10	26	84·4	16·5	20·5/36	7·7	2·9/12
6-group	4- & 3-groups	14	22	60·6	24·0	13·3/36	9·4	5·8/12

[*Continued overleaf*

(* The denominator indicates the total possible in that task.)

CHILDREN

5-group	4-group	—	25	49	13·9	4·7/25	5·0	6·9/10
5-group	4- & 3-groups	1	24	60	27·2	8·4/25	4·7	4·6/10
6-group	4-group	10	26	85	20·4	23·3/36	6·6	2·5/12
6-group	4- & 3-groups	14	22	74	19·3	19·0/36	7·2	2·7/12

TABLE 4.6

On a simple triad-learning and relearning hypothesis, it is difficult to see why the performance on the 5-task, when it follows only the 4-task, should differ from that *which we get when it follows the 4 and the 3*, as indeed it does in the case of the children. There is no difference in the case of the adults.

When the 6 immediately following the 4 is compared with the 6 following the 4 and the 3, we see that in the case of the adults there is a markedly poorer performance in the (4)6 case than in the (4, 3)6 case. It is possible that this could be explained in terms of the smaller amount of learning and relearning demanded in the (4, 3)6 case, though for the reasons given above this is likely to be balanced out by other factors militating in the opposite direction.

3. PERFORMANCES ON THE 7-GROUP UNDER DIFFERENT TREATMENTS

If we compare results on the two different treatments of the 7-task, it will be seen that there is not much difference to be predicted here, nor to be observed in the case of the adults (Table 4.7). The predictions are not justified, however, by the results of the children, who obtain better scores on the (5)3 treatment than on the (3)5 treatment.

Task	*Previous experience*	*S*	$R_1+R_2+R_3+N$	*A Op.*	*S.D.*	*B Op.*	*S.D.*	*Equations**
ADULTS								
7-group	4-, 3- & 5-groups	14	35	56	21·2	9·6	5·9	5·7/12
7-group	4-, 5- & 3-groups	19	30	53	19·7	11·7	6·8	5·1/12

(* The denominator indicates the total possible in that task.)

TRANSFER

CHILDREN

7-group	4-, 3- & 5-groups	14	35	67	24·3	23	6·6	3·7/12
7-group	4-, 5- & 3-groups	19	30	50	9·9	15	7·8	4·9/12

TABLE 4.7

4. PERFORMANCES ON THE 9- AND 9A-GROUPS COMPARED

The tables below show the expected relationships of difficulty between the 9- and 9A-groups, and the actual performance measures obtained.

Task	*Previous experience*	*S*	$R_1+R_2+R_3+N$	*A Op.*	*S.D.*	*B Op.*	*S.D.*	*Equations**
			ADULTS					
9-group	4-, 3- & 6-groups	3	78	45	25·9	9	12·9	7·6/12
9-group	4-, 6- & 3-groups	4	77	74	24·2	20	14·7	6·1/12
9A-group	4-, 3- & 6-groups	15	66	59	29·4	18	22·0	6·8/12
9A-group	4-, 6- & 3-groups	15	66	68	24·4	30	20·2	2·6/12
			CHILDREN					
9-group	4-, 3- & 6-groups	3	78	77	14·0	42	21·7	4·8/12
9-group	4-, 6- & 3-groups	4	77	95	24·5	37	25·1	2·3/12
9A-group	4-, 3- & 6-groups	15	66	81	23·2	54	13·1	2·9/12
9A-group	4-, 6- & 3-groups	15	66	71	17·4	46	16·9	3·5/12

(* The denominator indicates the total possible in that task.)

TABLE 4.8

When we give the nine game after the two different treatments, (4, 3)6 and (4, 6)3, it is evident that on the triad analysis we should not expect any differences in performance. In fact, the nine game after the (4, 3)6 seems appreciably easier than when it follows the (4, 6)3. This applies both to children and adults, but the difference is more marked for the adults.

Comparing the performances of adults and children

I. DIFFERENTIAL EFFECTS OF THE 'FITTINGNESS' OF VARIOUS STRUCTURAL RELATIONSHIPS

We shall begin by looking at the situation when subjects do the 3-group, followed by the 6-group, followed by the 9-group. We shall use the same measures of transfer: the overall performance on the 3-, 6- and 9-groups as compared with the overall performance on the 6-, 3- and 9-groups, on the one hand; and the overall performance on the 3- and the 6-groups as compared with the overall performance on the 6- and the 3-groups, on the other hand.

It will be remembered that there are two groups of subjects that had the 3-group followed by the 6-group, and two groups of subjects that had the 6-group followed by the 3-group. This is because in one case the third task was the cyclic 9-group, and in the other case the '3-by-3' group which we have labelled 9A. Mean performances for these combined larger groups will be given, where applicable.

2. ADULTS AND CHILDREN COMPARED ON THE 3-, 6- AND 9-GROUPS

ADULTS			CHILDREN		
A Operation		*S.D.*	*A Operation*		*S.D.*
(3)+(6)+(9) =	125	50·7	(3)+(6)+(9) =	180	37·2
(6)+(3)+(9) =	178	40·3	(6)+(3)+(9) =	214	52·7
(3)+(6) =	80	27·3	(3)+(6) =	102	26·9
(6)+(3) =	104	22·9	(6)+(3) =	119	34·4
(3)+(6) =	92	34·7	(3)+(6) =	103	35·7
(6)+(3) =	106	18·4	(6)+(3) =	94	27·8
B Operation		*S.D.*	*B Operation*		*S.D.*
(3)+(6)+(9) =	24	20·2	(3)+(6)+(9) =	64	27·8
(6)+(3)+(9) =	43	16·3	(6)+(3)+(9) =	66	25·4
(3)+(6) =	15	4·8	(3)+(6) =	22	7·3
(6)+(3) =	22	5·6	(6)+(3) =	29	5·6
(3)+(6) =	15	11·2	(3)+(6) =	21	10·0
(6)+(3) =	22	10·0	(6)+(3) =	22	8·4
Equations			*Equations*		
(3)+(6)+(9) =	20		(3)+(6)+(9) =	13	
(6)+(3)+(9) =	15		(6)+(3)+(9) =	9	
(3)+(6) =	13		(3)+(6) =	8	
(6)+(3) =	9		(6)+(3) =	7	
(3)+(6) =	10		(3)+(6) =	8	
(6)+(3) =	8		(6)+(3) =	11	

TABLE 4.9

3. TREATMENTS COMPARED

Treatment

ADULTS

	(6–3)		S.D.	(3–6)		S.D.
A	(6) + (3) + (9) =	178	40·3	(3) + (6) + (9) =	125	50·7
	(6) + (3) =	104	22·9	(3) + (6) =	80	27·3
B	(6) + (3) + (9) =	43	16·3	(3) + (6) + (9) =	24	20·2
	(6) + (3) =	22	5·6	(3) + (6) =	15	4·8
E	(6) + (3) + (9) =	15		(3) + (6) + (9) =	20	
	(6) + (3) =	9		(3) + (6) =	13	

CHILDREN

A	(6) + (3) + (9) =	214	52·7	(3) + (6) + (9) =	180	37·2
	(6) + (3) =	119	34·4	(3) + (6) =	102	26·9
B	(6) + (3) + (9) =	66	25·4	(3) + (6) + (9) =	64	27·8
	(6) + (3) =	29	5·6	(3) + (6) =	22	7·3
E	(6) + (3) + (9) =	9		(3) + (6) + (9) =	13	
	(6) + (3) =	6		(3) + (6) =	8	

TABLE 4.10

4. ADULTS AND CHILDREN COMPARED ON 9A-GROUP

		ADULTS		CHILDREN	
			S.D.		S.D.
A	(3) + (6) + (9A)	157	57·1	184	54·7
	(6) + (3) + (9A)	174	41·0	165	43·7
B	(3) + (6) + (9A)	33	27·9	75	20·3
	(6) + (3) + (9A)	52	26·9	68	22·5
E	(3) + (6) + (9A)	17		11	
	(6) + (3) + (9A)	10		15	

TABLE 4.11

Let us examine in these summary tables the differences between the performances of children and adults. If we consider first the (3)6 treatment, there are two scores, one including the scores on the 9-group and one not including them. When the 9 scores are included, the adults perform very much better than the children. If we restrict ourselves to the score on the 3-task and the 6-task, there is a similar trend, but it is much smaller.

Turning to the (6)3 treatment, if we include the scores on the 9-group, there seems to be a difference between the children and the adults; but if we exclude the 9 scores, there is little, if any, difference. This is a similar phenomenon to that observed with (3)5 and (5)3, only in that case it was somewhat attenuated. No doubt, giving the 5-group in preparation for the 3-group is presenting children with an easier task than giving them the 6-group in preparation for the 3-group.

We may summarise the differences between children and adults on (3)5, (5)3, and (3)6, (6)3, as follows:

Adults perform better than children on the (3)5 treatment.
Adults and children perform very much the same on the (5)3 treatment.
Adults perform better than children on the (3)6 treatment.
Adults and children perform very much the same on the (6)3 treatment.

In addition to comparing adults and children, we can also compare children with children and adults with adults on the different treatments. Children fare better on the (5)3 treatment than they do on the (3)5 treatment, whereas adults' performances are approximately the same for both. Children do approximately equally on (6)3 and (3)6, but adults do better on the 3(6) treatment than on the 6(3) treatment. So it seems that the differential between the performance of children and adults is the same in the (3)5, (5)3 situation, as it is in the (3)6, (6)3 situation, but the differential between the orders of presentation is not equal for children and adults.

We might at this point recall what happened in the case of (2)4 and (4)2 (as reported in our first volume, *Thinking in Structures,* 1965). We have summarised these order-effects in Table 4.12. Part (I) is to be read in columns. For example, the (2)4 column means that the children and adults performed equally well on (2)4. From the (3)5 column, we can see that the children performed less well than the adults, and so on. In Part (II), the pairs of symbols are to be read horizontally. For example, we could say that among the children the (2)4 section performed less well than the (4)2, as shown by the first pair in the top line. The last pair on the bottom line shows that the adults performed better on (3)6 than on (6)3. Part (III), giving performance on the B Operation in terms of percentages, reveals the same picture.

(I)

CHILDREN/ADULTS COMPARED

	(2)4	*(4)2*	*(3)5*	*(5)3*	*(3)6*	*(6)3*
Children	=	=	−	=	−	=
Adults	=	=	+	=	+	=

(II)

SHALLOW/DEEP TREATMENTS COMPARED

Children	−	+	−	+	=	=
Adults	=	=	=	=	+	−

(III)

PERCENTAGE CORRECT ON B OPERATION

	Adults	*Children*
5 without 3 given first	60%	61%
5 with 3 given first	64%	35%
6 without 3 given first	26%	18%
6 with 3 given first	46%	27%

TABLE 4.12

We shall now compare the tables for the (2)4/(4)2 situation with those for the (3)5/(5)3, and so on. It is clear from Table 4.12 (I), based on A Operation scores, that in the (2)4/(4)2 situation children and adults are very much the same. When we turn to the (3)5/(5)3 situation, the adults have the advantage in (3)5, but are still even with the children in (5)3. They have the advantage in (3)6, but are even with the children once more at the (6)3 level. It is probable that this degree of equality between adults and children would change in favour of the adults if the complexity of the task were sufficiently increased. The second table,

Part (II), also based on A Operation scores, shows that for the children (4)2 is better than (2)4, and (5)3 better than (3)5. The adults, however, performed equally well in (4)2 and (2)4, and in (5)3 and (3)5. When we pass on to (3)6 and (6)3, the children perform equally in (3)6 and (6)3, but the adults perform better at the (3)6 level. In other words, the children who start off at the deep end have an advantage over their fellows who start off at the shallow end. This advantage they keep until they reach the (3)6/(6)3 level, when the two approaches become even. The adults start even at the (2)4/(4)2 level, that is, at the 'simple' end of the scale, but there is an advantage for those who start at the shallow end at the (3)6/(6)3 level. Whether this is a developmental phenomenon or due to adults being conditioned in their learning to prefer starting from the simple and going on to the more complex, it is not possible to say.

An interpretation of the results when transfer effects and task difficulty are considered in terms of structural relationships

The last two tables indicated the differential effect of the shallow end and the deep end treatment as we increased the degree of complexity of the two tasks. In structural terms, there are various ways in which the complexity of the task may be increased. We have already mentioned two ways: putting in more recursive thinking, and putting in more thinking of the embeddedness or overlapping types. We can also increase the number of elements in the group, which is likely to increase the difficulty of the task (although this is not certain). Whether a structure appears more complex or less complex probably depends on the way in which the subject formulates the rules governing it.

As we have built into the experimental design ways to control the variation and extent of recursion and the extent of embeddedness, we can draw some comparisons between the effects of recursive learning and embeddedness learning. For example, we can compare the total number of errors on a (3)5 sequence with the total number of errors on a (3)6 sequence. This would compare a simple recursive generalisation from (3)6, coupled with the embeddedness of the 3 in the 6.

SCORES ON THE A OPERATION

	3–5	*S.D.*	*3–6*	*S.D.*	*6–3*	*S.D.*	*5–3*	*S.D.*
CHILDREN	88	37·1	103	31·6	106	33·8	60	20·5
ADULTS	64	30·5	86	31·4	105	20·7	59	20·3

[*Continued overleaf*

	5–7	S.D.	6–9	S.D.	3–9	S.D.	3–9A	S.D.
CHILDREN	127	51·3	151	23·6	123	35·2	85	26·4
ADULTS	106	43·2	103	47·5	94	27·5	89	36·0

	6–9	S.D.	6–9A	S.D.
CHILDREN	151	23·6	155	44·7
ADULTS	103	47·5	129	48·3

TABLE 4.13

Although the increased number of triads encountered in the (3)6 situation, compared with the number encountered in the (3)5 situation, might be expected to lead to a greater number of errors, it is unlikely that a very large discrepancy between the two learnings could be accounted for solely by the relatively small triad discrepancy. In the tables above, for instance, the (6)3 contains almost twice as many errors as the (5)3, both for the children and the adults. The components of this difference are, first, the score on the five or six game and, second, the score on the three game. Now we know that the error score on the six game is almost twice that on the five game, both for adults and children. But when the three game follows the six game, the errors are twice as many as when it follows the five game, both for adults and children. It seems, therefore, that being presented with the 3-group after the 6-group, which presumably can only be facilitated if it is realised that the 3-group was previously met embedded in the 6-group, is a much harder task for both children and adults to cope with than learning a 3-group as a particularisation of a previously encountered cyclic 5-group. Why this is so we can only speculate. Probably, when a subject learns the 5-group or the 3-group on the machine, he relies to some extent on the symmetry about the neutral element. This helps him to transfer both 5 to 3 and 3 to 5. This symmetry is not so marked in the 6-group, since there are three elements on one side of the neutral and two on the other. Structurally, too, the 6-group is very different from the 3-group, to a greater extent than the 3-group is different from the 5-group. Both the 3-group and the 5-group are straight cycles without any subgroups. It is true that the 3-group and the 6-group are also both cycles, but this is not easily noticeable. The 6-group also has two subgroups, a 2-group and a 3-group. It can be generated as a direct product of the 3-group by the 2-group, so that its structure is very different. It seems that the move from this type of structure to a simpler but different structure is a more difficult feat than to move from a symmetrical-looking cyclic group to a smaller edition of the same kind of structure.

In each of these cases, it should be possible to predict the number of errors in one task from the number of errors in the other, on the basis of the ratio of the number of triads to be learned. In the (5)3 treatment, thirty-four triads must be learned, and in the (6)3 treatment, forty-five. So the ratio of the errors on the S–R hypothesis of learning by rote would be 34:45. The actual ratio is 50:86, which does not differ significantly.

We can also investigate the differential effect between the (5)7 and the (6)9 treatment. In this case we are comparing a pure recursion exercise with an overlapping plus recursion exercise. The 6- and 9-groups do overlap in the 3-group, and there is also a recursive increase from a 6-cyclic to a 9-cyclic. In this case, also, we find that the overlapping increases the difficulty, but more so for the children than for the adults. Whether this is due to recursion or to extra difficulty caused by the overlapping, it is not possible to say. We can make some interesting comparisons of treatment of the (3)9 and the (3)9A as it affects adults and children.

ADULTS		S.D.	CHILDREN		S.D.
(A) (6+9)	= 103	47·5	(A) (6+9)	= 151	23·6
(A) (6+9A)	= 129	48·3	(A) (6+9A)	= 155	44·7
(B) (6+9)	= 23	19·52	(B) (6+9)	= 61	26·2
(B) (6+9A)	= 35	22·3	(B) (6+9A)	= 72	19·1
(E) (6+9)	= 14		(E) (6+9)	= 8	
(E) (6+9A)	= 12		(E) (6+9A)	= 5	
(A) (3+9)	= 94	27·5	(A) (3+9)	= 123	35·2
(A) (3+9A)	= 89	36·0	(A) (3+9A)	= 85	26·4
(B) (3+9)	= 22	15·2	(B) (3+9)	= 40	23·6
(B) (3+9A)	= 31	21·3	(B) (3+9A)	= 48	17·6
(E) (3+9)	= 12		(E) (3+9)	= 7	
(E) (3+9A)	= 8		(E) (3+9A)	= 11	

(A)=A Operation score;
(B)=B Operation score;
(E)=Equation score

TABLE 4.14

If we look at Table 4.14 we see that the adults and the children on the 3+9A treatment are very much the same on the A Operation; and yet on the 3+9 treatment the adults are distinctly superior, both on the A and the B Operations. In other words, replacing multiple embeddedness by simple embeddedness, and by a rather hefty piece of recursion, 'throws' the children. This effect is summarised separately in Tables 4.15 and 4.16.

ADULTS

	3+9	*S.D.*	*3+9A*	*S.D.*		
(A)	94	27·5	89	36·0	3+9 same as 3+9A	*Overall effect*
(B)	22	15·2	31	21·3	3+9 better than 3+9A	3+9 better
(E)	12		8		3+9 better than 3+9A	than 3+9A

CHILDREN

(A)	123	35·2	85	26·4	3+9 worse than 3+9A	*General trend*
(B)	40	23·6	48	17·6	3+9 better than 3+9A	3+9 worse
(E)	7		11		3+9 worse than 3+9A	than 3+9A

TABLE 4.15

We may summarise the A Operation performances also in the following way:

	3+9	*S.D.*	*3+9A*	*S.D.*
ADULTS	94	27·5	89	36·0
CHILDREN	123	35·2	85	26·4

TABLE 4.16

A somewhat different effect can be observed with (6)9 and (6)9A. Here there is overlapping instead of embeddedness: the 3-group overlaps four times between 6 and 9A, and once between 6 and 9. With 6 and 9A we have done away with recursion, whereas with 6 and 9 we have kept it in. It seems that for the children the advantages of *multiple* overlap are counterbalanced by the disadvantages of recursion, and they score about even. The adults, who are able to engage in recursive thinking, that is, able to generalise more readily, find the (6)9 treatment easier to tackle than the (6)9A treatment.

Let us now have another look at the relationship between (6)3/(5)3 and (3)5/(3)6 (Table 4.13). In (6)3/(5)3 we are comparing embeddedness with particularisation, that is, with recursion, and in each case from the deep-end point of view. In (3)5/(3)6 we are comparing a recursion which is a generalisation with an embeddedness, but in each case from the shallow end. What we find is that deep end plus embeddedness is a harder task than deep end plus recursion. Yet shallow end plus embeddedness is only slightly harder than the shallow end plus recursion. In psychological literature on transfer, it is generally accepted that a difficult-easy order results in greater positive transfer than an easy-difficult order. What our work has shown is that it is not simply a question of the order, difficult-easy or easy-difficult, but also of the inner structure of the two tasks. This question needs to be further investigated.

If we compare the (3)9/(3)9A table with the (6)9/(6)9A, we can see from the first of these tables that recursion by a factor, that is, 3 proceeding to 9, is harder for the children than multiple embeddedness. For the adults, recursion by a factor is about even with multiple embeddedness. When we look at the Equation scores, the adults' (3)9 performance is better than their (3)9A. With the children, there is a slight tendency the other way round. In other words, recursion by a factor is somewhat easier for the adults than embeddedness, whereas the converse is the case for the children. The table also gives us some information about the functioning of overlap as compared with combined recursion and overlap. We can see on the overall performance of the A scores that the children on recursion with simple overlap, that is, on 6 to 9, do about as well as children on multiple overlap, that is, on 6 to 9A. The adults, on the other hand, do rather better on recursion with simple overlap.

If we compare the performance on the (5)7 order of tasks with that on the (6)9 order of tasks (Tables 4.13 and 4.14), there is some suggestion that the (6)9 order is slightly more difficult for children, although this does not reach a significant level. Indeed, the Equation score shows that it disappears altogether. As far as the adults are concerned, there is no difference between the two, either on the A Operation or the Equation scores. Now, on a simple stimulus-response rote-learning theory, which assumes that this task consists essentially of learning a set of triads, in the (5)7 task there are 74 triads to be learned, and in the (6)9 task 117. But the actual performance on these tasks is not in the proportion of 74 to 117, and departs significantly from what would be predicted on an S–R learning theory. We would suggest that here is another piece of evidence that, in seeking to understand the learning of tasks and the transfer between tasks, it is important to take into account not simply the amount of rote-learning that has to take place, though this is undoubtedly an important factor, but also the functional relationships between the structures which the tasks embody.

As we have studied the differences between adults and children on the various performance scores, it has become reasonably clear that, whenever recursions (particularly up to the higher order groups) are involved, the adults do considerably better than the children. This can be seen on the (5)7, (6)9, (3)9 and (6)9A scores. These all involve, to a greater or lesser extent, recursions, embeddedness and overlapping. If we examine the same data directly for differences between adults and children, the pattern is somewhat difficult to discern, since there are several variables operating at once and it is not easy to keep any of them constant. We have already noted that the extent of recursion and the order of tasks both influence the differential between adults and children. The extent of embeddedness also seems to be of importance. If we take the tasks in which a total of 220 instances (that is, 80 on one task, plus 140 on the other task) were encountered by both adults and children, and arrange them in order of difference between adults and children, starting with the highest difference *in favour of the adults,* we get the following order:

(i)(3)9, (ii)(3)5, (iii)(3)6, (iv)(6)3, (v)(5)3, (vi)(3)9A.

Let us offer a provisional explanation why this should be so. In (3)9, we have a recursion by generalisation by six elements as opposed to simple embeddedness. In (3)5, we lose the embeddedness (which works differentially against the children), but the extent of recursion is reduced from an increase of 6 to an increase of 2. So it seems that the large amount by which the recursion increment is reduced, as between the (3)9 series and the (3)5 series, makes the differential in favour of the adults less in (3)5 than in (3)9. In (3)6, embeddedness is introduced (which favours the children) although recursion is slightly increased from two elements more to three elements more. In these first three cases, the shallow end principle is employed, that is, the task begins with the least complex one. In (6)3, we have recursion by particularisation by three elements, i.e. we are applying the 'deep-end' policy, which favours the children. Simple embeddedness is preserved. In other words, the only difference between (3)6 and (6)3 is the order of the task, which favours the children and therefore reduces the differential between adults and children. In (5)3, we further reduce the extent of recursion from three elements to two elements; we also keep the 'deep-end' functioning, but there is no further embeddedness. Dispensing with embeddedness might be expected to militate against the children, but the reduction of recursion would be even more in their favour. We thus have a slight differential improvement in favour of the children in this case. In (3)9A, we have a switch to the shallow end (which favours the adults); on the other hand, we have no recursion (which favours the children), and there is also quadruple embeddedness (which greatly favours the children). On balance, the children actually score better than the adults, although not significantly so.

It might be possible to give some kind of quantitative measure to recursion, overlapping, embeddedness, and the extent of 'deep-end' approach. The recursion score would be simply the difference between the number of elements in the two tasks in a series. The embeddedness score would be the number of times the one group was embedded in the other. The overlapping score would be the number of times a common part of both structures occurred as an isomorphic image in at least one of the structures. To arrive at a total score, measuring the extent to which the adults have an advantage over the children, one could take twice the recursion score, plus twice the overlapping score, minus the embeddedness score, and minus three if the difficult task was done first. This produces a very similar ranking to that produced by the Equation scores (Table 4.17). The rank correlation coefficient is in the region of +0·9. It is not seriously suggested that such an *ad hoc* 'formula' can explain anything; it merely enables one to estimate the combined effect of the influences that tend to increase or decrease the differential performances between adults and children. What the 'formula' expresses in words is that

(a) recursion and overlapping operate in favour of the adults;

(b) embeddedness and starting with the more complex task operate in favour of the children.

EQUATION SCORES (AS PERCENTAGES)

	3–5	*3–6*	*6–3*	*5–3*
CHILDREN	46	40	51	74
ADULTS	70	55	43	75

[*Continued overleaf*

	5–7	*6–9*	*3–9*	*3–9A*
CHILDREN	38	33	39	58
ADULTS	58	59	58	59

	6–9	*6–9A*
CHILDREN	33	21
ADULTS	59	49

TABLE 4.17

5. DISTRIBUTION OF 'SUCCESSES' AND 'FAILURES' AMONGST ADULTS AND CHILDREN

If we take 90 per cent or more correct responses on the B Operation as a criterion of 'knowing' a group, we can split up our subjects into those above the 90 per cent mark and those below it. We could also consider obtaining half or less than half correct responses on the B Operation as 'failing to know a group', and split our subjects on this score as well. When we do this, we get the following distribution of 'successes' and 'failures' between adults and children:

	Successes	*Failures*
ADULTS	22	9
CHILDREN	3	24

TABLE 4.18

These are taken on the final task in a series, namely the 9-, 9A- and 7-groups. One might inquire whether success on the final task bears any relation to the way in which subjects tackled it. A reasonable strategy would be for the subject to try all the different combinations as uniformly as possible, in order to find out what the outcomes are. If one finds a narrow concentration on certain sets of cells in the matrix, one might expect a poor performance on the B Operation. One might therefore expect a low variance on the frequency scores for the successful subjects and a high variance for the 'failures'. Measuring the variances on the frequency matrices and the percentages correct on the last task given to each subject, we have for the adults:

Mean variance of 'successful' subjects = 173
Mean variance of 'failure' subjects = 225

From a detailed study of the performance of the three 'high variance' subjects amongst the successes, it is apparent that one of these repeated 'neutral against neutral resulting in neutral' one hundred times in a row (perhaps he was an 'infuriated subject', who was obliged to continue to the end of the 140 trials in spite of having learned the task), another applied the neutral operator twenty-two times against neutral and against X_1, and concentrated another thirty plays on three cells in the X_1 column. In these cases, the rules of the experiment were producing 'freak' results. If these two subjects are omitted from the 'successes', the mean of the variances on the frequencies comes to 118 instead of 173.

The difference is even more dramatic with the children. The 'successful' variance is again in the 100 region, but the 'failures' average a variance of 358. It seems that

(a) successful subjects tend to concentrate on spreading their inquiry more evenly over the matrix than the failures;
(b) adults spread their inquiries more evenly than children.

If we look at the frequency variances of the 'in-between' subjects, we obtain a mean of 215, which is very close to 225. It seems, therefore, that a low variance in the frequency does sort out the good B Operation performers, i.e. those in the upper 10 per cent, from the rest.

It would be interesting to see whether, by comparing the frequency matrix, the position matrix and the error matrix of each subject, we were able to devise an index of ability to extrapolate from previously learned structures or, as some would say, of insightful behaviour. One way of doing this would be to select subjects from whose frequency matrices it is clear that, on a given element played against all other elements in the matrix, they have made either one or no errors. When this stringent criterion is applied, we discover that there are only five subjects doing 9-tasks (i.e. either 9 or 9A) who satisfy it on three or more columns of the matrices. Four out of these five are amongst the upper 10 per cent of 'successful' subjects. The fifth one also comes in the upper 10 per cent on the 9A score, and comes second on the overall score for his group of subjects. It seems that this criterion does select certain of the successful subjects, although there are many other successful subjects that do not meet its requirements.

Salient points from the chapter on transfer

(a) The existence of a variety of structural relationships between mathematical groups makes it possible to study how such relationships differentially affect performance in transfer situations. The relationships studied are recursion (which includes both generalisation and particularisation), embeddedness, and overlap.

(b) We have used three basic measures to study the effects of transfer: the A Operation, which is the number of errors made in the course of the initial learning session; the B Operation, which is the number of errors made in a test phase in which all the possible state-operator combinations are presented and a prediction of the outcome is required; the Equation score, which is a measure of the subjects' *understanding* of the rule structure of the group he has learned.

(c) It is possible to set up various models to explain what is being transferred in the learning of a series of tasks of this kind. One model is based on stimulus-response theory and assumes that the essential task facing a subject is to learn a set of stimulus–response–outcome associations. Another model of a more cognitive type regards the subject's main task as learning the roles of the different operators and the rules generating the group. Each of these models can be further subdivided into narrow and wide S–R type explanations, and narrow and wide role-explanations.

(d) It is possible to evaluate the difficulty of successive tasks on the basis of these four models. We predict how difficult one task should be, as compared with another, by assessing it on each model in turn. By referring to the actual performances of the subjects, we can see which explanation handles the data most economically.

(e) On the stimulus-response-outcome association learning model, we may label each cell in the matrix as follows:

S completely the *same*: same stimulus, same response, same outcome as in the equivalent cell of the previous task,
R_1 relearning type 1; new stimulus, same response, same outcome,
R_2 relearning type 2; same stimulus, new response, same outcome,
R_3 relearning type 3; same stimulus, same response, new outcome,
N completely *new*; new stimulus, new response, new outcome.

(f) It is evident that:

(i) children consistently find it more difficult to generalise than adults,

(ii) children consistently find it easier to particularise than to to generalise,

(iii) children find the difficult-easy (5)3 treatment easier to handle than the (3)5 treatment.

(iv) on the (3)5 treatment adults do better than children, but on the (5)3 treatment the performances of the adults and children approximate.O n an S–R–O model there should be no difference between the 5-task under the two conditions, 5 preceded by 3, or 5 given first—but there is,

(v) on the (3)6 order, the adults again perform better than the children, and once again the performances of adults and children approximate on the (6)3 order,

(vi) adults and children both find embeddedness much harder than generalisation,

(vii) adults and children both find overlap more difficult than generalisation,

(viii) where multiple embeddedness, e.g. (3)9A, is replaced by simple embeddedness and recursion, e.g. (3)9, the narrow margin between adults and children becomes much bigger,

(ix) recursion by a factor is much harder than multiple embeddedness for children, i.e. (3)9 is much harder than (3)9A,

(x) adults find recursion by a factor, (3)9, easier than multiple embeddedness, (3)9A.

(g) A variance measure which reflects the evenness of distribution of a subject's plays over the whole matrix can be computed, and it is evident that the mean variance of the 'successful' subjects is consistently and considerably less than the 'unsuccessful' subjects. This difference is very marked with the children.

5

Psychological implications

The basic presupposition upon which our experiments were based was that the different formal relationships (in the mathematical sense) between the tasks to be learned would be important factors in determining the ease of learning a series of such tasks; and, furthermore, that the *way* the tasks were learned would also be influenced by the structural interrelationships between tasks. This, of course, assumes that, in addition to learning a set of 'stimulus–response–outcome' triads, the subjects were also learning something about the regularities or rules determining the nature of the triads. But, it may be asked, do we need to make this further assumption about something being learned in addition to the S–R–O triads? Although the experiments were not specifically designed to answer this question, we believe that, by making appropriate analyses of the component parts of the learning of each task, we can go some way towards giving an answer. What this amounts to is an attempt to evaluate the relative explanatory efficiency of associationist and structural theories of learning.

We may briefly recapitulate the four models considered in Chapter 4 as follows:

(a) Narrow S–R model. This assumes that only the S–R–O triads learned in the immediately preceding task determine learning in the present task.

(b) Extended S–R model. This assumes that the S–R–O triads of all the previously performed tasks determine learning in the present task.

(c) Narrow role model. This assumes that the subject has discovered that certain stimuli (play panel symbols) played against certain responses (state panel symbols) consistently bring about certain outcomes. Thus the subject has learned one or more disconnected codes or rules which help him to predict the outcomes correctly.

(d) Wide role model. This assumes that the subject has learned that all the stimuli are related to the responses and outcomes in consistent ways, and that these consistent relationships can be expressed by a very small number of rules. This model is an advance on (c) because, by relating

NARROW S–R MODEL

Task	Preceded by	New	New plus relearning	Adults: Mean A Op.	Adults: Mean B Op.	Adults: % B Op.	Children: Mean A Op.	Children: Mean B Op.	Children: % B Op.
5	4–3	21	24	52	4·0/25	16·00	60	8·4/25	33·60
6	4–3	27	29	60·6	13·3/36	36·95	74	19/36	52·78
7	4–5–3	26	29	53	11·7/49	23·88	50	15/49	30·61
7	4–3–5	24	30	56	9·7/49	19·59	67	23/49	46·94
9	4–6–3	65	77	74	20/81	24·69	95	37/81	46·68
9	4–3–6	65	78	45	9/81	11·11	77	42/81	51·85
9A	4–6–3	45	66	68	30/81	37·04	71	46/81	56·79
9A	4–3–6	45	66	59	18/81	22·22	81	54/81	66·67

EXTENDED S–R MODEL

Task	Preceded by	New	New plus relearning	Adults: Mean A Op.	Adults: Mean B Op.	Adults: % B Op.	Children: Mean A Op.	Children: Mean B Op.	Children: % B Op.
5	4	—	25	48	5·3/25	21·20	49	4·7/25	18·80
5	4–3	1	24	52	4·0/25	16·00	60	8·4/25	33·60
6	4	10	26	84	20·5/36	56·94	85	23·3/36	64·72
6	4–3	14	22	60·6	13·3/36	36·94	74	19/36	52·78
7	4–3–5	14	35	56	9·6/49	19·59	67	23/49	46·94
7	4–5–3	19	30	53	11·7/49	23·88	50	15/49	30·61
9	4–3–6	3	78	45	12·9/81	15·93	77	42/81	51·85
9	4–6–3	4	77	74	14·7/81	18·15	95	37/81	45·68
9A	4–3–6	15	66	59	18·0/81	22·22	81	54/81	66·67
9A	4–6–3	15	66	68	30·0/81	37·04	71	46/81	56·79

TABLE 5.1

the rules identified in (c), the subject has increased the efficiency of his coding system so as to be able to predict correctly all or most of the time.

These four models, the first two of which are associationist and the second two structural, imply different views of what is being transferred from task to task.

Let us first assume that an associationist model is adequate to account fully for the subject's behaviour. On this assumption, we can assess the amount of learning involved in each task and rank their difficulty accordingly. This we did in Chapter 4, and now reproduce the results in summary form in Table 5.1, together with the mean performance based on the A and B Operation scores. Table 5.2 presents the Spearman correlation coefficients between task difficulty, as assessed on the two associationist models and the two performance measures we have called the A and B Operation scores. Two things may be noted. First, that only one of the eight coefficients reaches a normally accepted level of significance (5%). Second, that the correlation coefficients for the children's performances were consistently and substantially higher than the adults. From these observations it would seem reasonable to conclude that the associationist models are not sensitive predictors of task difficulty and that, if anything, the children behave more according to associationist learning models than adults do. The latter point is not surprising and fits in well with other findings.

As we examine Table 5.1 it is the *departures* from expectations based on the associationist models which stand out much more than the agreements. Looking first at the Narrow S–R model, we see that, whilst the task difficulty ranges from twenty-four to thirty triads (new plus relearning) on the first four tasks listed, the performance measures on the B Operation, in the case of adults, range from 16 per cent to 37 per cent.

	ADULTS		CHILDREN	
	A	*B* %	*A*	*B* %
Narrow S.R.	+ ·205	− ·065	+ ·759	+ ·410
Extended S.R.	+ ·024	− ·336	+ ·483	+ ·245

TABLE 5.2

Similar trends, though less marked, occur in the children's results. Again, if we compare the 9-task preceded by 4, 6 and 3, with the 9-task preceded by 4, 3 and 6, and also with the 9A-task preceded by 4, 6 and 3, the 'new plus relearning' column ranges only from 77 to 80, whilst the performance for adults ranges on the A Operation from 45 to 74 and on the B Operation from 11 per cent to 37 per cent. In this instance, the departure from expectation, whilst marked for the adults, is negligible for the children.

If we compare the first four tasks on the Extended S–R model, we see that each involves approximately the same amount of 'new plus relearning', yet performance on the B Operation ranges from 16 per cent to 57 per cent in the case of the adults, and a similar trend is seen in the children's results.

Finally, whilst there is in general an almost fourfold increase in task difficulty, as assessed on these models, none the less the performance in terms of errors on the A Operation varies relatively little. Indeed, if we compare performance on the 5-task with that on the 9-task when preceded by the 4-, 3- and 6-tasks, we see that task difficulty according to the Extended S–R model increases from 24 to 78 items, but performance shows an *improvement* from 52 errors to 45 errors.

All these departures from expectations based on associationist models suggest that, in addition to the S–R–O triads, something more has been learned. It is this 'something more' which the structural models proposed below can better take into account.

Before leaving our consideration of the S–R models, however, it is interesting to see how far they can predict the differential effectiveness of learning some parts of the tasks as compared with others. To what extent can these associationist models help us to understand *the way* in which tasks are learned, rather than the difficulty of learning them? We must refer back to our labelling of the cells of the matrices based on S–R interpretations which were given in Chapter 4, pages 83–88 inclusive. Since in some cases the number of cells labelled R_1, R_2 and R_3 is small, we may for our present purpose pool these three types of cell on the grounds that they all involve some type of relearning. We might then reasonably expect that the incidence of errors should increase as follows: fewest in the cells where the S–R–O combinations are identical with those in previous tasks (labelled *S*); next fewest in the cells which entail the learning of new and hitherto untried S–R–O combinations (labelled *N*); and most in the cells which entail some unlearning of previously learned associations and the learning of new associations (labelled R_1, R_2 and R_3).

The table below (Table 5.3) shows the incidence of errors on each task in these three categories. It is evident that the prediction of steadily increasing error-incidence from *S* to *R* is not in general substantiated.

Indeed, it is difficult to pinpoint any consistent patterning in the way errors are made. There does not even seem to be a consistent tendency to make fewer errors on the *S* cells than on either the *N* or the *R* cells, which is most surprising. We must conclude that these associationist models are not helpful in understanding how component parts of a complex task are learned.

We turn now to a consideration of the more structural models which we have called the narrow and wide role interpretations of learning. It will be recalled that in every task there are certain role structures which are 'the same'. For instance, there is a neutral element, which when

Mean errors per subject per cell on B Operation

	S	*N*	*R*	*A.=Adults* *C.=Children*
3 preceded by 4	0·12	0·13	0·18	A.
	0·31	0·27	0·22	C.
3 preceded by 5 or 6	0·16	—	0·00	A.
	0·22	—	0·09	C.
5 preceded by 4	/	0·24	0·19	A.
	/	0·21	0·16	C.
5 preceded by 4 and 3	0·09	0·19	0·18	A.
	0·22	0·21	0·41	C.
7 preceded by 3 and 5	0·04	0·20	0·37	A.
	0·29	0·44	0·68	C.
6 preceded by 4 and 3	0·34	0·42	0·39	A.
	0·52	0·48	0·54	C.
6 preceded by 4	0·54	0·61	0·57	A.
	0·60	0·69	0·65	C.
9 preceded by 6 and 3	0·40	0·28	0·11	A.
	0·37	0·48	0·29	C.
9 preceded by 3 and 6	0·00	0·12	0·10	A.
	0·67	0·50	0·52	C.
9A preceded by 6 and 3	0·36	0·40	0·38	A.
	0·33	0·57	0·76	C.
9A preceded by 3 and 6	0·19	0·26	0·31	A.
	0·43	0·72	0·71	C.

TABLE 5.3

acting as an operator induces no change in the existing state of the machine. There is another way in which all the tasks are alike on the role interpretation. If the subject selects a play whose symbol is placed at the same distance from the neutral as the symbol in the window at that time, but on the opposite side, the outcome will be neutral. We have called the area of the matrix covered by these two rules the *constant role area* or the *C cells*. We have called *E cells* those where there is a combination of symbols which has not been met with previously but whose role is the same and has only to be extrapolated to the new symbols. *G cells* are those in which a role, met with in a previous task, will result in correct predictions if generalised to the new task. Cells labelled *R* are those where the role previously learned must now be relearned.

We can now examine the error distribution on the narrow role interpretation. We might well predict that the lowest incidence of errors would be on cells in the common role areas (*C*), and on those cells where simple extrapolation enables correct predictions to be made (*E*); and the greatest incidence of errors either on the Generalisation (*G*) or the Relearning (*R*) cells. (We have no theoretical basis for predicting which of these last two types of cells is likely to show the greatest incidence of errors.) Let us, then, compare the *C* and *E* mean errors with the *G* and *R* mean errors, and predict that in each case the *C* and *E* error incidence will be less than the *G* and *R* error incidence.

The table below shows the actual incidence of errors (Table 5.4).

Task	*C*	*E*	*G*	*R*	*A.=Adults* *C.=Children*	*Prediction supported or not*
5 preceded by 3	0·04	0·06	0·31	0·14	A.	+
	0·19	0·17	0·54	0·33	C.	+
7 preceded by 3 and 5	0·04	0·02	0·38	0·29	A.	+
	0·29	0·24	0·72	0·69	C.	+
7 preceded by 3	0·05	0·07	0·36	0·33	A.	+
	0·00	0·04	0·49	0·44	C.	+
9 preceded by 6 and 3	0·16	0·10	0·34	0·36	A.	+
	0·40	0·42	0·50	0·49	C.	+
9 preceded by 3 and 6	0·06	0·02	0·15	0·20	A.	+
	0·44	0·22	0·62	0·64	C.	+

TABLE 5.4

It is evident that the results consistently support the view that subjects learn in terms of the narrow role learning model. Let us now go further and inspect the performances of individual subjects, in case by taking the mean performances for groups of subjects we may have masked some information. We may ask, for example, how many subjects in each group made more errors, on the average, on *C* and *E* cells than on *G* and *R* cells. The picture that emerges is set out below.

Mean errors per cell on B Operation for individual subjects

ADULTS: 7 preceded by 5 and 3

Mean on C+E	*Mean on G+R*	*G+R mean>C+E mean*
0	·47	+
·05	·43	+
0	·06	+
·26	·53	+
0	·53	+
·11	·60	+
0	·37	+
0	·10	+
·05	·10	+

CHILDREN: 7 preceded by 5 and 3

0	·20	+
0	·06	+
0	·50	+
0	·62	+
·21	·81	+
0	·33	+
0	·50	+
0	·77	+
0	·53	+

ADULTS: 7 preceded by 3 and 5

Mean on C+E	*Mean on G+R*	*G+R mean > C+E mean*
0	·63	+
·08	·50	+
·12	·21	+
0	·04	+
·04	·50	+
0	·04	+
0	·40	+
·04	·75	+
0	·08	+
·12	·75	+
0	·04	+

CHILDREN: 7 preceded by 3 and 5

·60	·88	+
·28	·67	+
·24	·83	+
·16	·67	+
·48	·46	+
·20	·75	+
·12	·25	+
·32	·71	+
·16	·75	+

ADULTS: 5 preceded by 3

·08	0	−
0	·58	+
0	·25	+
·23	·50	+
0	·33	+
0	·17	+
0	·33	+
0	0	=
0	0	=
·23	·83	+
0	·08	+

CHILDREN: 5 preceded by 3

Mean on C+E	*Mean on G+R*	*G+R mean+G>E mean*
·69	·75	+
0	·33	+
·15	·58	+
0	·33	+
·08	·25	+
·46	·67	+
0	·67	+
0	·42	+
·23	·58	+

ADULTS: 9 preceded by 6 and 3

·30	·86	+
·14	·32	+
·05	·14	+
·22	·14	−
·03	·14	+
·03	·14	+
·08	·32	+
·38	·86	+
·14	·41	+
·11	·25	+

CHILDREN: 9 preceded by 6 and 3

0	·25	+
·41	·45	+
·14	·39	+
·27	·39	+
·89	·89	=
·78	·95	+
·19	·30	+
·86	·66	−
·08	·25	+

ADULTS: 9 preceded by 3 and 6

Mean on C+E	*Mean on G+R*	*G+R mean+G>E mean*
·30	·68	+
0	0	=
0	0	=
·03	·27	+
0	·02	+
·14	·36	+
0	·02	+
·03	·16	+
0	·07	+
0	0	=

CHILDREN: 9 preceded by 3 and 6

·43	·91	+
·35	·43	+
·68	·89	+
·89	·89	=
·51	·93	+
0	0	=
·22	·55	+
·14	·43	+
·19	·59	+

This more detailed examination of individual subjects' performances only serves to underline the fact that the mean performances listed in the earlier table faithfully reflected the performances of most of the subjects and were not the result of excessive error-making in the predicted direction by a few subjects.

It could, of course, be asked whether the probability of making an error in a particular cell of the matrix in the B Operation does not simply indicate the frequency with which the S–R–O combination was chosen to be played by the subject during the A Operation. If this were the case, we should expect the combinations played most frequently in the A Operation to show the fewest errors, and this would support an S–R interpretation of learning rather than the structural model at present under consideration. We can check this by calculating the mean frequency of play of each category of cell for any particular game during the A Operation. When we do, we discover that in fact the

S–R–O combinations in the *C*, *E* and *G* cells played most frequently also show the most errors, the converse of our S–R prediction. Table 5.5 below compares the mean frequency of play in the A Operation of the *C*, *E*, *G* and *R* cells with the mean frequency of error-making on the same cells on the B Operation. It is worth noting that, on the structural model, the natural prediction is that, as soon as the subject discovers the role of a *C* cell to be the same as in a previous task, he will logically play that cell no longer but concentrate on the *E*, *G* and *R* cells, perhaps distributing the frequency of his plays in that order. From the table it looks very much as if this is what happened.

Task		*C*		*E*		*G*		*R*	
		A play frequency	*B error frequency*	*A*	*B*	*A*	*B*	*A*	*B*
5 preceded by 3	A.	4·30	0·04	4·68	0·06	6·34	0·31	9·23	0·14
	C.	5·68	0·19	4·63	0·17	5·12	0·54	10·61	0·33
7 preceded by 3	A.	1·68	0·05	1·70	0·07	3·49	0·36	5·06	0·33
	C.	2·59	0·00	2·75	0·04	2·81	0·49	5·17	0·44
7 preceded by 5	A.	2·27	0·04	2·15	0·02	4·49	0·38	3·50	0·29
	C.	2·95	0·29	3·26	0·24	2·45	0·72	3·37	0·69
9 preceded by 3 & 6	A.	1·80	0·06	1·57	0·02	1·51	0·15	2·82	0·20
	C.	1·70	0·44	2·12	0·22	1·55	0·62	2·07	0·64
9 preceded by 6 & 3	A.	1·56	0·16	1·28	0·10	1·79	0·34	2·78	0·36
	C.	1·97	0·40	1·81	0·42	1·40	0·50	2·20	0·49

TABLE 5.5

A similar table (Table 5.6) presents the mean frequency of play of cells labelled *S*, *N* and *R* according to the S–R interpretation of learning, and the B error frequency for these same cells. Again, there is no evidence to suggest that combinations played most frequently in the A phase of the task present the lowest number of errors in the B phase of the task, when the cells are labelled according to an S–R interpretation.

These analyses constitute further evidence that, in addition to the learning of disconnected S–R–O combinations, there is a higher level type of learning, which we have called structural learning.

Task		S		N		R	
		A play frequency	*B error frequency*	*A*	*B*	*A*	*B*
5 preceded by 3	A.	8·70	0·09	6·41	0·19	5·06	0·17
	C.	9·56	0·22	5·86	0·21	5·22	0·40
7 preceded by 5	A.	2·26	0·04	4·43	0·20	4·09	0·37
	C.	3·05	0·29	3·56	0·44	2·32	0·68
9 preceded by 3 & 6	A.	2·48	0·00	4·90	0·12	5·35	0·11
	C.	1·96	0·67	1·69	0·50	1·48	0·45
9 preceded by 6 & 3	A.	1·90	0·40	1·67	0·28	1·22	0·13
	C.	3·22	0·37	1·73	0·48	1·62	0·29

TABLE 5.6

How these two aspects of total learning may be interrelated forms the subject of a speculative model to be presented in a later section of this chapter. First, however, we must examine one further piece of evidence in favour of the view that structural learning was taking place.

Differential effects of fittingness of symbolisation to structures

When designing the symbols to represent different elements in the mathematical groups used as our experimental tasks, we built in certain perceptual cues, which, if used, would help the discovery of how earlier tasks were structurally related to later tasks. For example, there are two 'obvious' subgroups in the 9A-task (see diagram, page 124). One is represented by keeping the colour yellow constant and varying the shapes between triangle, circle and square; this we shall call the *inner subgroup*, as its elements are clustered around the neutral, which is represented by the yellow circle. The other subgroup is represented by keeping the circle shape constant and varying the colours between orange, yellow and red, to form the 3-cycle; this we shall call the *outer subgroup*.

One might consider differences in the amount learned in these two subgroups and other 'comparable' parts of the matrix: one might also consider the subgroups where no perceptual constant is provided. The remaining parts could, for example, be the following:

(r) where red responses are given to red stimuli
(o) where orange responses are given to orange stimuli
(tr) where triangle responses are given to triangle stimuli
(sq) where square responses are given to square stimuli
(res) parts of the matrix not covered by any subgroup or other category.

The (*r*) and (*o*) parts of the matrix could be used as controls to check against the learning of the 'yellow' subgroup; the (*tr*) and (*sq*) parts of

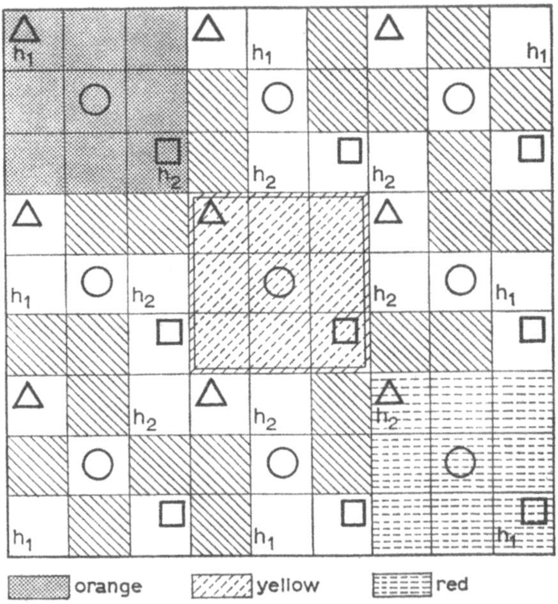

9A break-up (showing subgroups)

the matrix could be used as controls to check against the learning of the 'circle' subgroup, and of the (*res*) part, which is the residue.

In order to study these effects quantitatively we shall consider the differential results on the B Operation scores based on different parts of the matrix, to see whether our attempt to bring out the structure of the tasks by symbolisation has had any appreciable effect on learning.

Below is a table (5.7) for the break-up of the 9A-matrix into subgroups, constant colour sections, constant shape sections, and the residue: the numbers are to be interpreted as the probability of making an error on the B Operation in the part of the matrix indicated.

	Inner (yellow)	*Outer (circle)*	*Outer (hybrid)* (*h1*) (*h2*)	(*o*)	(*r*)	(*tr*)	(*sq*)	*Res.*
Children 9A preceded by 6 & 3	0·383	0·333	0·494, ·408 $\bar{x}$ = ·451	0·581	0·618	0·778	0·815	0·608
Children 9A preceded by 3 & 6	0·432	0·346	0·566, ·496 $\bar{x}$ = ·531	0·667	0·593	0·742	0·729	0·732
Adults 9A preceded by 6 & 3	0·32	0·28	0·35, ·39 $\bar{x}$ = ·37	0·45	0·38	0·49	0·20	0·456
Adults 9A preceded by 3 & 6	0·148	0·198	·297, 0·259 $\bar{x}$ = ·278	0·296	0·309	0·322	0·296	0·302

TABLE 5.7

We can group together the inner (yellow) and the outer (circle), because in each of these there is a perceptual invariant together with a subgroup with which it coincides. In the yellow subgroup this invariant is the colour yellow, in the circle subgroup it is the circular shape. Next we can take the 'hybrid' subgroups, i.e. where we have the structure of a subgroup, but without the perceptual invariant. Next come the cases in which the colour is invariant but no subgroup is apparent; next, the cases where the shape is invariant but still no subgroup is apparent; and, finally, the residue. We then obtain the following picture (Table 5.8).

Here again, the numbers are to be interpreted as the probability of errors being committed in the categories given.

It is not altogether surprising that, where the subgroup structure is brought out by a perceptual aid, either in the form of a constant colour (yellow) or of a constant shape (circle), the error-probabilities should be lowest. Again, it is not very surprising that the adults' error probabilities are everywhere lower than those of the children, even though in many cases there is not a great deal of difference.

Now, on a purely perceptual hypothesis one might argue that the

	Subgroup with perceptual invariant	*Subgroup without perceptual invariant*	*Perceptual invariant, but no subgroup (colour)*	*Perceptual invariant, but no subgroup (shape)*	*Residue*
Children 9A preceded by 6 & 3	·358	·451	·600	·797	·604
Children 9A preceded by 3 & 6	·389	·531	·630	·735	·82
Adults 9A preceded by 6 & 3	·30	·37	·44	·35	·371
Adults 9A preceded by 3 & 6	·173	·278	·303	·309	·267

TABLE 5.8

same error-probabilities should be expected every time the colour played is the same as the colour of the symbol in the window, particularly since the 'shape scheme' is the same in all three cases. This, however, is not so. When yellow is played against yellow, the error-probabilities are everywhere consistently lower than if red is played against red, or orange against orange. The only reasonable explanation for this is:

(a) that the yellow states and operators form a group,
(b) that all subjects have previously encountered this group, i.e. the 3-group, though in the framework of *different symbols*.

Some kind of transfer is evidently taking place which can reasonably be attributed to the recognition on the part of the subjects of the 3-structure, already learned; or at least previously encountered by them.

Let us now see what happens if, instead of withdrawing the subgroup structure and keeping the colour or shape constant, we withdraw the perceptual constancy of the symbols, but keep the subgroup structure. In the 9A-group there are two subgroups, namely

$$(y_2, 1, x_2) \text{ and } (y_4, 1, x_4),$$

in which both the shapes and the colours are varied. We can see, by looking at the probability tables, that the error-probabilities increase in almost every case, but not by so much as they do when we remove the group structure and keep the perceptual constants.

The one exception is the adults' Group (3)9A, who for some unaccountable reason seem to find the combinations of 'square' symbols very much easier than any other types of combination, with an error-probability as low as 20 per cent. On this particular task they appear, in fact, to be behaving more in conformity with the kinds of predictions that could be made on S–R assumptions than on structural assumptions, although the trend seen with the children is still observable.

We can observe that keeping the colour constant is easier than keeping the shape constant, assuming that no structural 'aid' is provided. This is in line with findings in other experiments. The trend is most clearly noticeable with the children, who are known to be better at colour than at shape discrimination. An adult has had so much practice with both that the differences are minimal, if indeed they exist at all.

The adults do not appear to find the residue any more difficult than the other parts of the matrix, with the exception of the part in which they are helped both perceptually and structurally. The children, however, particularly those who had the (6)9A treatment, find the residue almost impossible to learn, since an 82 per cent error-probability would roughly be what they would get if they knew nothing at all. The (3)9A children, however, only have a 60 per cent error-probability in this area. It is possible, as has already been suggested, that the embeddedness of the immediately preceding task, i.e. the 3-group, is a help in sorting out not only the structure embedded, but also the residue. With the (6)9A-group, where there is overlapping instead of embeddedness, there is no such effect.

If we make a similar analysis of the 9A matrices, but based on S–R principles instead of structural relationships, we get the results summarised in Table 5.9. It seems that breaking up the 9A matrices in S–R terms does not give a very clear picture. All that one can say, in the case of the children and the (6)9A adults, is that the S-part is easier than the rest—in other words, that the reinforcing effect of meeting the same outcomes in certain triads makes those triads easier to learn. Hardly an epoch-making discovery! Apart from this, there are no trends worthy of comment.

S–R table for the 9A groups

	S	N	R_1	R_2	R_3
Children 9A preceded by 6 and 3	·33	·56	·74	·81	·72
Children 9A preceded by 3 and 6	·42	·73	·72	·75	·68
Adults 9A preceded by 6 and 3	·39	·40	·39	·42	·27
Adults 9A preceded by 3 and 6	·18	·28	·25	·36	·24

TABLE 5.9

A possible theoretical model

We have presented evidence which we believe supports the view that, when subjects are required to learn the properties of mathematical groups that are embodied in an electrical machine, their method of learning can be most elegantly interpreted by a model which asserts that structural learning is taking place in addition to simple S–R learning. Whilst we should not expect to find pure examples of any of the four possible models we have described, we might none the less expect some subjects to approximate increasingly to one or other of them. For example, we might expect increasing approximations to the wide role model as their familiarity with mathematical structures increased. In the early tasks, and possibly also in the early phases of later tasks, we should certainly expect some S–R learning to take place, in order to put sufficient information about component parts of the task into short-term storage for various methods of coding or structuring to be tried out. This is particularly likely because, it will be remembered, our tasks had to be handled without short-term memory aids like pencil and paper. In our previous study we showed that the overall success of subjects correlated with the strategies they employed. The most efficient strategy, which we called the 'operator strategy', led to the most orderly storage of information, because it involved the same operator being tested against a variety of states. The 'pattern strategy', a little less systematic and imposing a greater memory load, tried out operator-state-outcome combinations from a restricted part of the matrix. The last strategy, hardly worthy of the name, consisted of apparently random trials of any combination of operator-state and outcome.

In the experiments reported in this book it was essential, particularly as the tasks became more complex, for subjects to be systematic in their behaviour, so that the load on short-term storage could be kept to a minimum. This left as much cognitive capacity as possible free for trying out rules or codes which would provide a shorthand way of structuring and handling seemingly disconnected items. This interaction between short-term memory and the trying out of rules is reminiscent of Posner's conceptualisation of human thought. Posner (1965) claimed that a number of aspects of human intellectual performance, which have long resisted systematic investigation, can be examined analytically in terms of the transformation processes and retention involved. This approach to information-handling, according to Posner, is roughly analogous to viewing complex learning in terms of combinations of simpler S–R associations.

Posner brings together a wide range of tasks, hitherto treated separately by psychologists, all of which have in common the need to process information over time. He suggests a system of three main types of information-transformation, based upon the relation between the input and output required for perfect performance of the task. He first considers information-conservation tasks, in which the subject is required to preserve all the input information in his response. This sort of task has hitherto been studied most extensively by means of information measures. A typical example is the standard reaction-time task. His second type of task involves information-creation. Here, the classic example is word-association tasks, in which a simple stimulus leads to a train of responses which exceeds the information value of the input. It is, however, the third type of task, involving information-reduction, which is more relevant to our own experiments.

Posner distinguishes tasks such as addition, classification and selection, which require the subject to produce a subset of stimulus input in his output. Any task in which the subject is required to map more than one stimulus input on to a simple response is a reduction task. This approach seems closely related to Bartlett's (1958) three types of thinking. His 'closed system type I', in which the response is implicit in the stimulus input, is analogous to information-reduction; his 'closed system type II', which involves translation and in which there is a one-to-one correspondence between two coding systems, is analogous to information conservation; and his 'open system', which involves going beyond the information given, is analogous to information-creation. The particular relevance of all this to our present discussion lies in the approach to problem-solving. For Bartlett (1958) there is a 'point-of-no-return' which high level skills, such as thinking, share with perceptuo-motor skills. Beyond this point, the thinker is committed to a future direction of thinking, based on his processing of the items of information so far. Simon and Kotovsky (1963) similarly argue that 'if a subject is able to extrapolate a sequence, he holds in memory something different from the sequence with which he was presented. The sequence by itself provides no basis for its own extrapolation.' Thus the thinker must generate a pattern based on the transformed stimulus input. This represents exactly the combination of storage and information-transforms with which Posner is concerned.

As Posner (1965) puts it: 'Once a problem-solving task is viewed as involving both retention and transformation, the existence of a "point-of-no-return" follows as a natural consequence. This is so because the limitations on the amount of information which can be held in store force the subject to select information from the stimulus, relevant to the hypothesis upon which he is operating.' It is interesting, then, that Simon and Kotovsky (1963) find that the difficulty of their serial problems is most closely related to the number of items which must be held in store simultaneously if a subject is to infer the correct generating rule. And this means that, in any analysis of problem-solving, memory may be a limitation whenever a number of items must be integrated in order to produce the transformation which yields the solution.

Posner's experiments have certainly indicated the intimate relationship between thought and memory, and fit well with the sort of model of human information-processing developed by Broadbent (1958). On Broadbent's view, the human organism has a limited central capacity for processing information; if at a given time this capacity is taken up in one way, that amount of its capacity will not be available for other things. Applying this to our own findings, we can see that, if a subject regards the learning of a mathematical group as the storage of a number of items of disconnected information, that is, stimulus-response-outcome triads, there will be no capacity left to try out those very means of coding the information (Posner's information transforms), which, if successful, would appreciably reduce the load on memory. In fact, the four models we have explored are increasingly efficient in their potential for reducing the amount of information which has to be stored, and in replacing this memory-load by more and more widely applicable rules, which (with a minimum of information in store) can regenerate the whole mathematical group. No doubt, some simple rote-learning is essential if the subject is to hold enough items in short-term storage to be able to 'turn round on his own schemata' (Bartlett, 1932) and try out rules or codes which will reduce the information to manageable proportions. It may well be that starting with the more complex task first—i.e. 6 followed by 3 rather than 3 followed by 6, or 5 followed by 3 rather than 3 followed by 5—has the effect of forcing subjects quickly to abandon the attempt to solve the problem on the basis of memory alone and may accelerate the tendency to try out various coding mechanisms. Certainly, this view fits well with our findings in the experiments reported in *Thinking in Structures.* For instance, we observed that the overall performance on the 4-element group and the 2-element group was better when presented in the (4)2 order than in the (2)4 order. Likewise, we found a greater tendency to use higher order strategies (operator and pattern) amongst subjects thrown in at the deep end with the (4)2 order than with those let in gently with the (2)4 order. The same tendency has been observed in the present series of experiments in comparing the (3)5 order with the (5)3 order and the (3)6 order with the (6)3 order.

There is also evidence, presented earlier in this chapter, that the provision of perceptual cues can help the identification and learning of structural relationships, and that this can be effectively transferred from a narrower into a wider context, as when the 3-element group structure is found embedded in the 9-element group (which is a product of the 3-by-3 group).

Transfer effects

Whilst not intending to repeat here what we have already set out in detail in Chapter 4 about the possible effects of embeddedness, overlap and recursion upon transfer, we must indicate briefly how our results may be related to the other studies of structured learning of which we are aware.

It will be recalled that, where there was substantial embeddedness relating a larger group to an earlier, smaller group, this had the effect of narrowing the gap between the performance levels of the adults and the children, in favour of the children. Conversely, where there was substantial generalisation relating the structures of a smaller to a larger group, this tended to widen the gap between the performances of the adults and the children in favour of the adults. Is there anything in the normal developmental experience of children which indicates greater skill in spotting embedded structures than in correctly handling recursion by generalisation? In language development, small children generalise the tenses of irregular verbs and are surprised, perhaps even inhibited, when they discover how often these generalisations turn out to be incorrect. Moreover, as Chomsky and Miller have pointed out, structural embeddedness is a property of language which is met with constantly. By a relatively early age it may have become an overlearned skill. Could it be, therefore, that there is a large amount of positive transfer from language-learning to mathematics-learning, since in both cases facility with handling embedded structures leads to better performance and more rapid learning?

We may note that G. A. Miller has pointed out the limitations of verbal conditioning approaches to the study of language. As he says, this does not mean that the verbal conditioning explanation is incorrect but that it is only part of the story. There are other aspects of linguistic behaviour. This same point has been made with much supporting evidence in a quite different context by A. R. Luria (1961, 1966). Our own attempt to understand what is going on in the learning of mathematical structures has found a similar approach appropriate. After first trying to analyse the experimental results in S–R terms, we have eventually adopted a more structural approach which, whilst recognising that S–R connections must be established, takes account of higher order interrelationships. This structural approach seems to be forced on us when we try to account for the surprisingly high levels of performance of both adults and children on the more complex tasks given later in the series. In these cases, we regard the learning as based predominantly upon structural learning, and only to a very limited, though fundamental, extent on the learning of S–R associations.

In conclusion, we may note that in a book reviewing abstraction and concept formation, published four years after these experiments were begun, Pikas (1966) suggests three principles which he considers should guide future investigations in this field. Two of these are almost identical with those which guided the designing of our own experiments, namely, as Pikas puts it (p. 250):

1. The use of experimental material that is as original as possible and previously unknown to the Ss.
2. The employment of children as Ss to a greater extent.

It is significant that Pikas, working independently both of ourselves and of Posner, also drew attention to the role of memory in concept formation. Thus he writes (p. 231): 'To be sure, it has been said that "concept formation is affected by memory", but the present authors consider that, if research into the mechanism of concept formation is to make any progress in the future, it must start with an assumption that the function of memory tracks or storings or codes must occupy a central position in the working model.' What Pikas has said of concept formation of the traditional kind is also applicable to the learning of structures. Pikas's 'recoding hypothesis' is analogous to our 'structuring of the information held in short-term storage'.

One other general observation concerning the methodology of studying the learning of structures (and, for that matter, concept formation) is worth recording. We have seen that, if our measure of performance had been restricted to the total number of errors made in any phase of the task, we might have been tempted to conclude that an explanation in terms of an S–R model was more adequate than it is. It is only by analysing the component parts of subjects' performances that we begin to understand the *process* of learning rather than the degree of success or failure on a particular task. It is also only by such fine-grained analysis that we can critically evaluate the merits of competing theoretical explanations.

In this respect, we would include our model amongst the information-processing type models reviewed by Hunt (1962) and agree with him that whilst '. . . they do not provide us more parsimonious explanations of some data than previous models do . . . they do make more detailed predictions within a given setting'. In the case of our experiments it was only by examining in detail what was happening in particular cells of an overall matrix (the structure to be learned) that we were able to differentiate between S–R and structural type models and indicate what may have been occurring *between* input and output in the course of the learning of a structure. It is knowledge of this kind that we need if we are to understand the *process* of learning complex tasks sufficiently well to facilitate them in the classroom as well as in the laboratory. It is to some observations and speculations in this direction that we turn in our final chapter.

6

Educational implications

How are our experimental results likely to affect educational practice in the future? Let us take the relevant results in turn and discuss, first, whether their implications are taken into account in present educational practice, and secondly, if they are not, how this practice should be changed.

The first and the most obvious result of the experiments is that there are subjects who are able to tackle a series of tasks of this degree of complexity. At the outset, we had both wondered whether it was wise to stretch the complexity of the tasks so far. But the subjects were able to reach reasonable criteria on complex tasks like the 3-by-3 group, the cyclic 9-group and so on. What is more, there did not seem to be a very great difference between the performance of the children and that of the adults, and indeed, on certain types of presentation the differences were negligible. What are the implications of this? One obvious one is that children can learn with relative ease structures of much greater complexity than the ones now being presented to them. In the normal classroom situation a stimulus-response situation is established, and the stimuli are on the whole not systematically classified nor are relationships between the stimuli insisted upon. In short, structural learning is not encouraged. The tasks with which our subjects, both children and adults, were confronted were such that it was impossible to learn them on the basis of rote memory. In a 9-by-9 table, for instance, eighty-one stimulus-response-outcome triads would need to be learned. The fact that any learning took place, beyond what could be expected by random trial and error, shows that the subjects must in some way have systematised their stimuli, responses and outcomes into *relations*. Whether they did this consciously or unconsciously there is no need to speculate, since our criterion was simply their behaviour in coping with the tasks. If they were able to learn much more in one presentation than in another, we can conclude that one way of presenting a structure is more effective than another; and if the total number of stimulus-response-outcome triads is the same in each presentation, some other factor must have made the learning more effective.

Evidence which points in the same general direction comes from the break-up of the testing stage of the 9A task. The 9A or 3-by-3 task has a number of sub-structures built into it which are isomorphic to the 3-group. One of these has the same symbols as are used in the learning of the 3-group; there are other subgroups in which the symbols are different; there are sections which have the same symbols without being subgroups; and there are the rest, which have different symbols as well as a different structure. On the structural hypothesis, one would expect the probability of making an error to be least in the first kind and to increase as one went on to the other sections. This is, in fact, what happens. Naturally, using the same symbols as in the previous task helps subjects to avoid errors in the first subgroup. What is more interesting is that, in the subgroups where the symbols are changed, errors are less frequent than when the symbols are the same and the group structure is changed. There is thus some evidence that it is the group structure which is transferred. It seems that relearning a structure is harder than relearning a stimulus-response-outcome situation. By implication, it could be hypothesised that a structure 'sticks' better than a set of unstructured associates.

It should be noted that the structures were not presented to the subjects in any systematic way, because the subjects were free to choose their own responses and predictions to each stimulus. In other words, there was no predigested passing on of structures from the machine to the subjects. But when structural learning *is* attempted in the classroom, this sort of predigestion is precisely what happens. The system is organised by the text-book or the teacher, and this is supposed to be passed over to the children by a process known as 'teaching'. Naturally, very few children assimilate this kind of stimulus situation. The majority only learn in a very narrow way the kinds of responses they are expected to give to particularised groups of stimuli. The generalities of the predigested structural approach largely escape them. An example of such a predigested approach would be the learning of theorems. Another would be the doing of types of geometrical problems which are 'taught' by suggesting that they should be tackled in particular ways. Any other type of problem will be out of the children's range, even if the solution has the same overall structure.

There are, of course, a few children who, in spite of these pedagogical errors, nevertheless learn mathematics. This happens in spite of, rather than because of, the teaching we give them. Most mathematically enthusiastic children teach themselves, either through spare-time reading or through discussion with the teacher.

Now the subjects of our experiments had to form their own structures out of the relationships which were programmed into the machine. They were able to 'ask the structure' as many questions as they pleased by trying the various operators. In this way it was open to them to devise a strategy to build up the relationships in terms of which correct predictions could be made and the problems solved. This kind of random mathematical situation is not given to children to sort out in our present classroom practice. We suggest that such unsystematic situations ought to be introduced, so that the children may learn to create the systematisation themselves out of the disorder with which they are faced. The organisation of the data will be their own and become an integrated part of their model of the world around them. They will then be able to make predictions in a meaningful way, in the same way as they make predictions in everyday life.

Methods of introducing such situations are described in the volumes of the *Adelaide Program of Mathematics*. The programme is based on the children's own experience, acquired through the use of a large variety of materials. These are structured in such a way that even random play will induce a certain number of structural ideas in the children's minds. This is followed up by the use of instruction cards which suggest experiments for the children to do and ask questions about the conclusions they draw from these experiments. Eventually, abstractions are formed, and then further experiments are based on these abstractions. The series is still in course of construction, and is at present available from kindergarten up to seventh grade.

It will be recalled that, in explaining our experimental results, we made use of a variety of models. The main types were the stimulus-response-outcome model and the role (or structural) model. In the stimulus-response-outcome models, it was assumed that the children were learning to associate certain outcomes to certain pairs of stimuli and responses. The stimuli were defined entirely in terms of the perceptual data which reached the subjects' sense organs. The other type of model, the role model, suggested that the subject was learning to associate a *role* to a certain part of the structure; for example, he might correctly associate blue circle with causing a certain type of change in the state of the machine, and this would enable him to make a correct prediction of the outcome in every such case. This kind of association would not necessarily be permanent, but the subject would learn the roles that were being played for the time being by certain operators. These roles could then be associated in another learning task with a different perceptual stimulus. Thus the *whole role structure* would be the response to one perceptual stimulus which could be transferred to another perceptual stimulus. On the stimulus-response-outcome explanation, such a change of the stimulus percept would involve the relearning of all the stimulus-response-outcome triads, whereas on the whole role explanation no real relearning would be required. Again, in the reversal of simple to complex and complex to simple orders, no differences can be predicted in degree of difficulty on the stimulus-response-outcome theory. On the whole role theory, the complex to simple order would be expected to be the easier one, and this is what we actually find. In short, the whole role model gives in general a more accurate prediction of the subject's behaviour than the stimulus-response-outcome model.

The implications for educational practice are fairly obvious. If learning is tied to a particular symbol system, when this symbol system is disturbed everything has to be relearned. In order to achieve *insights of roles of operators within structures* it appears to be necessary to vary the symbol system and, if possible, also vary the physical situations in which the symbol system is applicable. In current mathematics teaching, we restrict children quite severely to one particular symbol system. In fact, mathematical experts regard it as extremely bad practice to 'confuse' children by using different symbols at different times for the same things. According to our present findings, the evidence points to the contrary. It might often be more satisfactory to allow children to develop their own symbol systems, to compare one symbol system with another, to have discussions about the relative efficiency of one system as against another. It would also be desirable to vary the situations in which the symbol systems are applicable, so that the roles are not associated with *particular* situations, but acquire a separate existence as abstractions which are part of an abstract structure. This principle has been formulated as the *principle of multiple embodiment*.

Some of the results concerned with generalising and particularising in the present series of experiments confirm those obtained in our earlier experiments (when only the two 4-groups and the 2-group were used as experimental structures). One is that children find it consistently more difficult to generalise than adults; and another, that they find it consistently easier to particularise than to generalise. Now the Geneva school has established that generalisation is more difficult for children than it is for adults. This is possibly because in a generalisation the internal relationships between structures need to be consciously realised. Children find much less difficulty in generating a structure than in thinking about relationships between structures. As for the greater ease of particularisation, this is in line with the findings in other experiments on transfer; if two tasks have to be learned, it is more advantageous to start with the difficult task and finish with the easy one.

Yet in current mathematical programmes, generalisation is the order of the day. It is automatically assumed that it is more effective to start with a simple structure and then to generalise progressively to more complex and presumably more 'difficult' structures. It is forgotten that, during this process, children have to look at the relationships between the structures. If they were presented with the most general structure first, assuming that it was within their mental capacity, they would find it much easier to particularise from this than to generalise from the simple structure. In the Adelaide programme, for example, children from the very beginning are taught to think in terms of different number bases and different powers of a base number. This enables them to come to grips with the idea of place value. The ideas of powers, bases and exponents are necessary preliminaries. Once they are grasped, place value as expressed in the decimal system becomes very much clearer and understandable. The total time taken is no greater, while efficiency is increased. The same principle is also applied higher up the mathematical scale. It has been found possible to start the algebra of integers by the study of vector spaces of more than one dimension. The study of positive and negative numbers becomes an easy matter when treated as a particularisation of a vector space. In fact, complex numbers are as easy as ordinary real numbers for children of ten or even younger. Children who have learned to handle the application of the cyclic 4-group to a two-dimensional vector space, and have consequently built the complex algebra, will more easily be able to handle the application of the 2-group to a one-dimensional vector space and so build the real algebra. This is partly because they have, in effect, built the real algebra in the course of building the complex algebra.

It is better to throw people in at the deep end of the mathematical pool, because then they will want to swim. If we let them enter at the shallow end, gingerly, they will try to walk. When they get out of their depth, they are liable to 'drown', mathematically speaking. Our results show that children do in fact find the treatment where the 5-group is given first and the 3-group afterwards easier to handle than where the order is reversed. This is true, whether the criterion is the total number of errors made in both tasks, or the total number of errors in the succeeding 7-group. If we compare adults and children, we see that the (3)5 treatment favours the adults, no doubt because it is a generalisation, at which adults do better. On the other hand, with the (5)3 treatment the adults and the children have about the same success in coping with the task. Whether this would be so with adults who had been brought up on the deep-end policy from childhood, it is impossible to say. At the moment, it seems that adults are very much geared to the simple–complex sequence. When adults are 'thrown in at the deep end', they do not know what to do because they are unaccustomed to such treatment. Children, on the other hand, are constantly meeting situations in life which are quite novel and 'deep-endish' for them, and so are used to learning how to cope with them. They are good at finding sub-situations in these novel situations. Adults have usually met all the kinds of situation they are going to meet; on the few occasions when they meet a new one, they are not so happy with the complex as with the simple. The same remarks apply to the (3)6 order as against the (6)3; the adults perform considerably better than the children on the (3)6, whereas adults and children are roughly equal on the (6)3.

It will be remembered that a distinction has been made between generalisation and embeddedness. Generalisation is simply the building up of a structure to a greater size while keeping the rules, in general, as before. The original structure may be included in the generalised structure, or it may not. For instance, though the 3-group is not included in the 5-group, the cyclic generation rule is very similar, the only difference being that the 3-cycle consists of three steps and the 5-cycle of five steps. If we build up the 3-cycle to a 6-cycle, we find that the 3-cycle is actually included in the 6-cycle. This means that there are two relationships which exist between the 3-group and the 6-group:

(a) *generalisation,* because the 6-cycle is simply a longer version of the 3-cycle;

(b) *embeddedness,* because the 3-group is a part of the 6-group, that is, there is a 3-group which is a subgroup of the 6-group.

Both adults and children find embeddedness much harder to tackle than generalisation. (The same applies to overlapping, of which embeddedness is a particular case.) This may simply be because nobody is systematically taught to handle relationships between structures, either in schools or even in universities. Only in logic are such things studied, and then usually in the most abstract form. When such difficulty is found in learning structures that are related by simple inclusion, embeddedness or overlapping, it must mean that something essential is missing from our educational practice.

In the Adelaide programme, sets are introduced from the beginning in such a way as to produce situations of overlapping, inclusion, identity and exclusion, and the corresponding logical relations are introduced at the same time. When the intersection of sets is introduced, the idea of the conjunction of the corresponding attributes which the members of these sets possess is also introduced. Similarly, when the union of sets is introduced, the idea of the disjunction of the attributes possessed by members of these sets is also introduced. In this way, 'set language' leads children to the understanding not only of adding and subtracting, but also of logical relations. Even four- or five-year-olds are able to construct Venn diagrams with three attributes, provided they are given a set of objects which possess all possible combinations of these attributes and of their negations. If, say, the attributes are 'large' and 'small', 'red' and 'blue', 'circle' and 'square', there will be eight objects, each of which possesses one particular combination of these attributes. A three-way Venn diagram can then be constructed. The children are told that each circle must contain only those objects which possess a particular attribute. For example, one circle might be for the *red objects*, the second for the *circles*, and the third for the *large objects*. Outside each circle must be placed all the objects not possessing the attribute which defines the set of things inside that circle. In this way, the whole universe of eight objects is divided into eight subsets, each consisting of one member. This would often not be a deep enough end in which to throw them in. In the Adelaide programme, on the deep-end principle, the set of objects consists of forty-eight members: three colours, four shapes, two sizes and two thicknesses. In addition, other attributes are used, such as those possessed by the children themselves (type of hair, colour of eyes, sex, and so on). In this way the situations are varied, and the multiple embodiment principle operates.

Although embeddedness is found difficult by children, differentially it favours them as against the adults. This is even more the case when there is multiple embeddedness. For example, if we take the 3-group and compare it with the 3-by-3 group we find that we have four images of the 3-group in the 3-by-3 group. It will be remembered that there is less of a margin between children and adults in the (3)9A treatment than there is in the (3)9 treatment. In the (3)9A treatment there is multiple embeddedness in the relationship, whereas in the (3)9 treatment there is recursion and simple embeddedness. The scaling down of the embeddedness and introducing of the recursion appears to decrease the advantage of the children over the adults. This suggests that embeddedness is not unsuitable for children to tackle. Perhaps, as we have remarked earlier, they are accustomed to it, whereas adults have become less accustomed. Certainly, children appear able to tackle a new situation more easily than adults, whatever the situation is, assuming that their previous experiences are equivalent. It is usually found that, when anything radically new is introduced into a mathematics programme, the children learn much faster than their teachers. This should not discourage the teachers, because there are bound to be children who are basically more intelligent than themselves. Consequently, if both start from zero, some children will proceed more quickly than the teacher. A younger and more elastic mind is *a priori* likely to tackle a new situation more effectively than an older and possibly more set mind.

Since children obviously prefer multiple embeddedness, whereas adults tend to lose this skill, embedding a structure is something we should pay more attention to, so as to preserve the ability to deal with this particular kind of relationship. Otherwise the only enduring relationship will be generalisation.

Up to now, very little has been done to help children to come to grips with logical relationships between structures. In the Adelaide programme, a great deal is made of finding structures in the sub-structure of other structures. In some of the work on geometry, where systems are studied almost in the abstract by a process of considering sets of colour, shape, and rotation operators, a great number of structures become known to children. These structures are represented by systems of arrows, with different types of arrows being used for different types of operators. The arrow structure is then axiomatised, that is, described in the most economical way, so that all relationships that can be established from the arrow system can also be established from the axioms. When this stage is reached, children are able to look at the systems directly and see the relations between them. Once a child has abstracted a number of systems from his own experience, has represented them by an arrow structure, and has finally established an axiom system, he is in a position to start the study of the relationships between these structures. This kind of work has been found quite practicable at the age of eleven in some experimental classes in Sherbrooke, Canada.

This work is being carried to its logical conclusions, that is, it is being expanded from systems treating mathematical groups to other systems treating *rings*. A second operation is introduced into a system by the establishment of isomorphisms or homomorphisms. For example, the Klein group has six isomorphisms of itself into itself (automorphisms). These can be used as an introduction to a 'second operation'. With cyclic groups, the set of homomorphisms in one group provides a second operation, which generates, together with the first operation, a structure known as a 'ring'. Other structural learning takes the form of a search for formal algebraical systems that give the rules for algebraic manipulations and so on. The enthusiasm of the children for this completely abstract structural work has to be seen to be believed. Nor is this the prerogative of the few intelligent children in a class. The less bright children are equally able to tackle the logical problems arising out of relationships between structures; the main difference is that they make more errors for a longer time, but they tend to be equally interested and equally willing. This part of the Adelaide programme is at a very experimental stage, but it is believed that eventually the study of relationships between systems will form an important part of the whole procedure. Perhaps it will bridge the gap between the elementary stage of learning, in which structures are built up, and the secondary stage, in which structures are compared and analysed.

Some of the classroom experimentation with structural learning is enabling us to formulate certain hypotheses. For example, it is possible that the ways in which structures have been presented were *too random*. In that case we have to find the optimum amount of systematisation in the presentation to occasion the maximum transfer. If the stimuli are too tightly organised, little transfer takes place; if they are too random, little learning takes place from which to transfer. It is suggested that the following order might be the most effective:

(1) Free manipulation of structured materials, constructed to embody certain relationships.

(2) 'Game'-like tasks in which rules are imposed and subjects asked to solve problems within the rule-structures. Variation of embodiment, keeping the same rules.

(3) Schematic representation of the rules (the constraints) by an

arrow-structure. This would represent the abstraction constructed.

(4) Establishment of an axiom-system from the study of arrow-structure. This would *analyse* the construction.

For example, we might take the following eight blocks:

and let children 'play' with them. This would be stage (1). Next the blocks can be placed as follows:

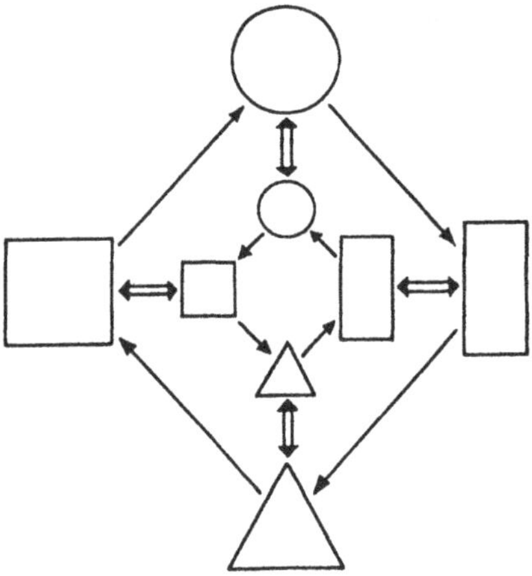

and a marker placed on one of the blocks. One problem would be to pass from a given block to another block in as few moves as possible. For example:

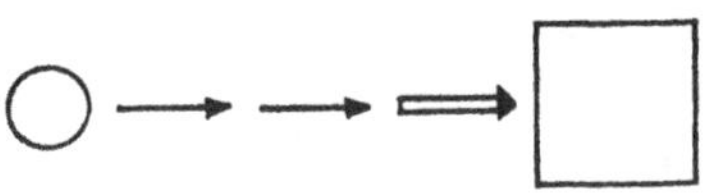

Or again, one can work out alternative routes, such as:

and

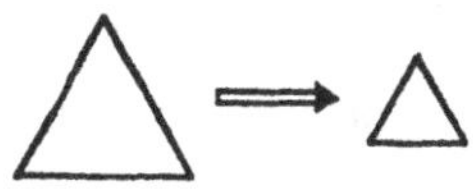

Alternatives provide equivalent routes and will be found to be equally interchangeable in every portion of the game. All possible routes are eventually placed in equivalence classes, represented in this case by the following 'shortest routes':

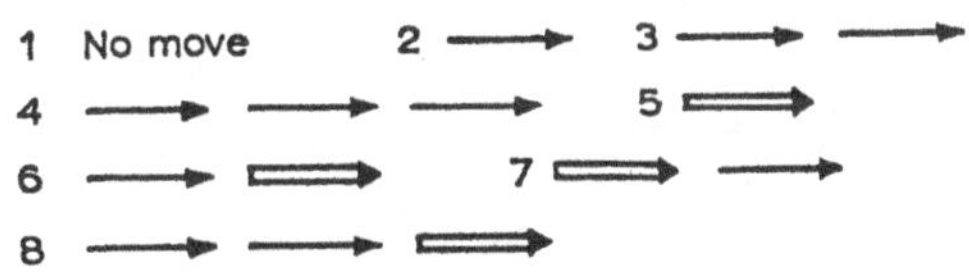

This leads very rapidly to the third stage, in which the arrow-structure is studied.

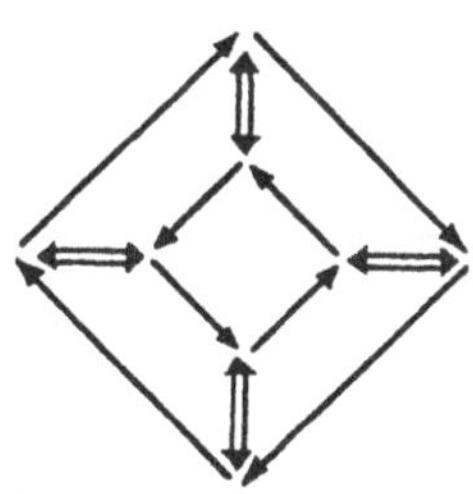

It may then be more effective to do another embodiment before passing on to the more 'abstract' stage. For example, using a square marked on one side with an A and on the other with a B, one could play a game isomorphic to the previous one by taking the two moves:

(*p*) flip the square over as though turning the page of a book,
(*q*) turn the square in its own plane a quarter turn clockwise.

The possible positions of the square would be represented thus:

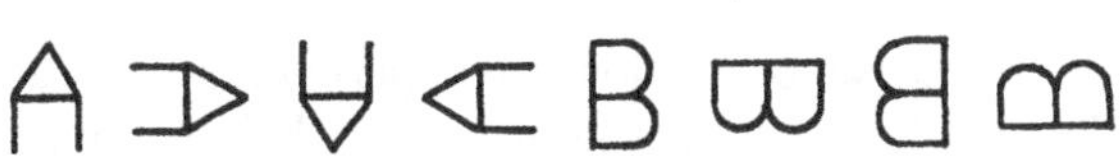

Now, provided A p B were true, problems of how to get from any position to any other position by means of p and q could be 'played with'. Equivalance classes of the routes could be established, and eventually a 'map of the game' drawn as

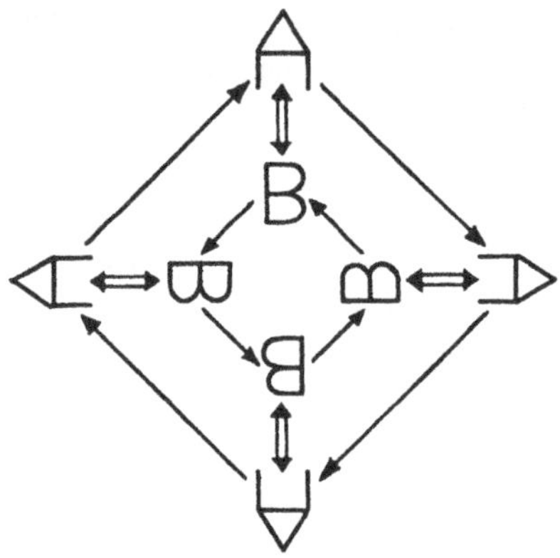

Then the axiom-system

1 → → → → = No move
2 ⇒ ⇒ = No move
3 → ⇒ → ⇒ = No move
4 ⇒ → ⇒ → = No move

could be established. Any of these moves could be introduced into a route, or suppressed from a route, without changing the equivalence class to which the route belonged.

Finally, the system could be 'played with' by proving 'theorems' like

→ ⇒ → belongs to the same class as ⇒

The 'proof' in this case would be:

→ ⇒ →
→ ⇒ → ⇒ → (introducing ⇒ ⇒ by 2)
⇒ (leaving out → ⇒ → ⇒ by 3)

It is easy to devise psychological experiments to study subjects' behaviour in handling axiom-systems. Their behaviour in embeddedness, overlapping and generalisation situations can also be investigated at all four stages of learning. An obvious hypothesis would be that learning tasks involving such relationships would become easier as the subjects progress through stages (1), (2), (3) and (4). Embeddedness can, very neatly, be 'seen' by comparing the arrow-maps of various structures. And ability to handle axiom-systems facilitates this kind of insight even more.

Readers interested in the detailed administration of such tasks in the classroom should refer to the *third* edition of Dienes' *Building Up Mathematics*.

References

BARTLETT, F. C. *Thinking,* Allen and Unwin (1958).

BARTLETT, F. C. *Remembering,* Cambridge University Press (1932).

BROADBENT, D. E. *Perception and Communication,* Pergamon Press (1958).

CHOMSKY, N., and MILLER, G. A. Introduction to the formal analysis of natural languages. In Luce, R. D., Bush, R. R., and Galanter, E. (Eds.), *Handbook of Mathematical Psychology,* Wiley, New York (1963), Vol. 2, pp. 271–321.

HUNT, E. B. *Concept Learning. An information processing problem,* Wiley, New York (1962).

LURIA, A. R. *Role of speech in the regulation of normal and abnormal behaviour,* Pergamon Press (1961).

LURIA, A. R. *Human brain and psychological processes,* Harper and Row, New York (1966).

MILLER, G. A. Some preliminaries to psycholinguistics, **20**, 15–20, *Amer. Psychol.* (1965).

PIKAS, A. *Abstraction and Concept Formation,* Harvard University Press (1966).

POSNER, M. I. Memory and thought in human intellectual performance, **56, 2** and **3,** 197–215, *Brit. J. Psychol.* (1965).

SIMON, H., and KOTOVSKY, K. K. Human acquisition of concepts for sequential patterns, 70, 534–46, *Psychol. Rev.* (1963).

For Product Safety Concerns and Information please contact our
EU representative GPSR@taylorandfrancis.com Taylor & Francis
Verlag GmbH, Kaufingerstraße 24, 80331 München, Germany